Sun Tzu's

THE
ART
OF
WAR

Plus

The Warrior's
Apprentice

A Student's Guide to
Winning at Anything

Gary
Gagliardi

Youth Non-Fiction
Book Award Recognition for
The Warrior's Apprentice

The Art of War Plus
The Warrior's Apprentice

Youth Nonfiction
Independent Publishers
Book Award
2006 - Semi-Finalist

This book also contains the only award-winning
translation of Sun Tzu's *The Art of War*

The Art of War Plus
The Ancient Chinese Revealed

Multicultural Nonfiction
Independent Publishers
Book Award
2003 - Winner

Award Recognition for *Art of War* Strategy Books
by Gary Gagliardi

The Golden Key to Strategy

Psychology/Self-Help
Ben Franklin
Book Award
2006 - Winner

*The Art of War Plus
The Ancient Chinese Revealed*

Multicultural Nonfiction
Independent Publishers
Book Award
2003 - Winner

*Making Money by Speaking:
The Spokesperson Strategy*

Career
Foreword Magazine
Book of the Year
2007 - Finalist

Strategy for Sales Managers

Business
Independent Publishers
Book Award
2006 - Semi-Finalist

*The Warrior Class:
306 Lessons in Strategy*

Self-Help
Foreword Magazine
Book of the Year
2005 - Finalist

Strategy Against Terror

Philosophy
Foreword Magazine
Book of the Year
2005 - Finalist

*The Ancient Bing-fa:
Martial Arts Strategy*

Sports
Foreword Magazine
Book of the Year
2007 - Finalist

*The Art of War
Plus Its Amazing Secrets*

Multicultural Nonfiction
Independent Publishers
Book Award
2005 - Finalist

The Warrior's Apprentice

Youth Nonfiction
Independent Publishers
Book Award
2006 - Semi-Finalist

Published by
Science of Strategy Institute, Clearbridge Publishing
suntzus.com scienceofstrategy.org

Third Edition
ISBN 978-1-929194-26-1 (13-digit) 1-929194-26-9 (10-digit)

Interior and cover graphic design by Dana and Jeff Wincapaw.
Original Chinese calligraphy by Tsai Yung, Green Dragon Arts, www.greendragonarts.com.

Publisher's Cataloging-in-Publication Data
Sun-tzu, 6th cent. B.C.
    [Sun-tzu ping fa, English]
    The art of war plus the warrior's apprentice Sun Tzu and Gary Gagliardi.
    p. 228 cm. 23
    Includes introduction to basic competitive philosophy of Sun Tzu
        1. JUVENILE NONFICTION / Social Issues / Self-Esteem & Self-Reliance.
        2. JUVENILE NONFICTION / Social Issues / Values & Virtues
        3. Military art and science - Early works to 1800.
    I. Gagliardi, Gary 1951— . II. The Art of War Plus Warrior's Apprentice
HD31.S764413 2000
658.8 /4 21 —dc19

Science of Strategy Institute/Clearbridge Publishing
2829 Linkview Dr. Las Vegas, NV, 89134
Phone: (702) 721-9631
garyg@suntzus.com
scienceofstrategy.org

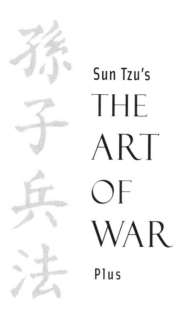

Sun Tzu's

THE
ART
OF
WAR

Plus

The Warrior's Apprentice

A Student's Guide to Winning at Anything

by Gary Gagliardi

Science of Strategy Institute

Clearbridge Publishing

Contents

The Art of War Plus
The Warrior's Apprentice

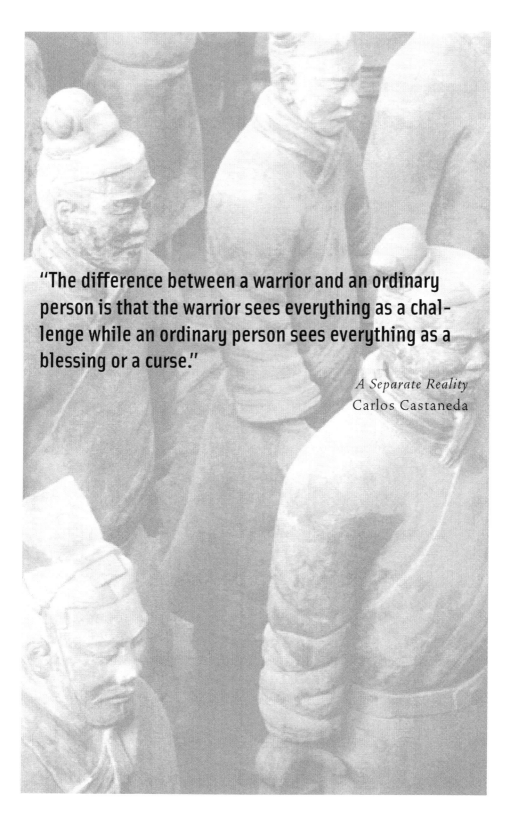

"The difference between a warrior and an ordinary person is that the warrior sees everything as a challenge while an ordinary person sees everything as a blessing or a curse."

A Separate Reality
Carlos Castaneda

Forward

Choosing to Win

Knowing how to win consistently is the secret art of strategy. In ancient China, Sun Tzu's powerful methods for good decision-making were restricted to the privileged. For over 2,000 years, the book you are about to read was banned to common people. Today, many if not most people would still like to ban this book because it teaches some dangerous truths. You are unlikely to find any copies of it in your school library.

It teaches you a kind of real, working magic, a magic that can help you find success in everything that you do.

These secrets for success were first written down 2,500 hundred years ago. Sun Tzu called these secrets 兵 bing-法 fa bing-fa. *Bing-fa* literally means "martial art." Its philosophy is the historical basis for all martial arts. However, he used *bing-fa* to mean all forms of competition. Sun Tzu wrote generally about all struggles within society and between people. Today, his methods are used to win in every type of competition, from business to sports to romance.

In discussing these contests, he teaches the use of only one weapon—the most powerful weapon of all—the human mind. Sun Tzu teaches that most people make the same basic mistakes in trying to win competitive contests without using *bing-fa*.

One of the biggest mistakes is mixing up competition with conflict. Competitive strategy, as defined by Sun Tzu, avoids conflict. Conflict only arises from failed strategies, not successful ones. *Bing-fa* teach you how to avoid conflict in getting what you want.

You don't do this by running away from challenges. Instead, you build "positions," which discourage people from challenging you. This is why Sun Tzu's strategy is called "winning without conflict."

In Sun Tzu's view, competition exists everywhere there is a choice. Competitive position exist in the minds of others. You build up winning positions by making good choices. His strategy is to make comparisons among alternative choices. Real competition takes place in the human mind. All alternatives choices are "at war" with each other within the human mind. His system is to control what goes on inside our own minds and the minds of others.

The purpose of this book is to make it easier for you to use Sun Tzu's idea in your life. As a young person and a student, you are taught to follow orders, but you don't win simply from following others. This book wasn't written for those who want to go through life as a warrior instead of a pawn.

The Power of Decisions

Why is Sun Tzu's system so powerful? Sun Tzu saw that our instincts are all wrong. When people are challenged, they react in one of two ways. Sometimes, they run away. Psychologists call this the "flight reflex." Other times, people attack those who threaten them. Psychologists call this the "fight reflex." Sun Tzu saw that neither flight (running away from challenges) nor fight (getting into battles) is successful over the long run.

People make these "flight" or "fight" decisions from instinct. To make other decisions, you must be trained in a better system of decision-making. You have to make better choices, but you have to make them instantly and automatically by trained instincts. A warrior wins, not because he is bigger, faster, or stronger than everyone else. A warrior wins because he knows how to do the right thing at the right time. This means make better decisions than others and making them faster. A warrior does at first what a fool does at last.

Warriors take control of their lives by making their own decisions. Our word "strategy" comes from the Greek word *strategos*, which means "the thinking of a commander." Warrior's win because they know how to take command themselves and others. Warriors know not only how to contributed as a member of a team, following directions, but also they know how to see opportunities and take advantage of them instantly.

This new type of thinking requires a different perspective. You need a way of seeing your options beyond flight or fight. Sun Tzu teaches the magical perspective of positioning. In his system, you continually focus on your position within a situation and how to improve it. You learn to see the world as a constellations of shifting positions rather than a series of unconnected events.

Positions are everywhere, hidden in everything. You have a unique position in the world. Because of that position, you have certain unique advantages and disadvantages. Once you understand your position, you can see opportunities that are available to no one else. Instead of fighting people, you move around them. Instead of running away from challenges, you seek to understand the opportunity that they represent. As you master the techniques of positioning, you constantly move toward your goals, avoiding situations in which you must fight or run away.

People misunderstand the true nature of winning. Winning isn't the end point in some contest except in children's games. In real life, winning is improving your position, moving it closer to making your dreams come true. Instead of thinking about your problems and your opponents, you must focus on the potential in your situation. Instead of fighting, strategy teaches you how to advance your position so that people cannot fight you—and ideally, over time, want to join you.

Strategically, both victory and defeat are similar. Each puts you in a new position. When you win your heart's desire—a prize, a love, or a promotion—you always discover that your real challenges are just beginning. Even when you fail to reach your goals, the knowledge you gain from the failure improves your position. Happiness never comes from where you are. The key to happiness is constantly making progress toward the horizon of your goals.

In martial arts, you don't simply push or strike your opponents, because if you do they will simply push and strike back. Instead, you examine your opponents' position. You look for opportunities to use your opponents' apparent strengths against them by catching them out of position. The use of physical leverage in martial art is exactly the same as the use of strategy in everyday life.

The secret is that strategy is a process, not a plan. It is a way of reacting, not an idea. Sun Tzu taught that planning alone does not work because the world is too complex, fast-changing, and unpredictable for rigid, long-term plans. Instead, strategy is a system for creating results under a wide variety of different circumstances. This requires the "warrior's mind," which uses a clear framework for resolving complex situations and choosing the right responses.

With the warrior's mind, you see the world in a different way. You recognize opportunities where you once saw problems. You look for answers instead of blaming others for your problems. When you are faced with a challenge, you can quickly analyze the threat, spot an opening, and act on your instincts.

The secret to winning is not just winning battles. For Sun Tzu, a "battle" is only a point of competition, a point of comparison, where a choice is made. "Fighting" means investing all your resources. Developing positions in advance enables you to win without fighting battles. Battles are expensive. If you can advance your position quickly and economically without fighting, you are better off. As you advance your position, strategy teaches you how to hold on to what you have won. You must be wary of "victories" that consume your time and energy but that fail to position you for long-term success.

The Hidden Code

As we said, *The Art of War* is written in a type of code. Half of this code is subtly revealed in the book's first chapter. There Sun Tzu explains the five key factors that define a strategic position. Then he says that deception is the basis of all warfare, signaling the reader that to understand the rest of the book, he or she must utilize those five key factors.

When you use the five-factors code to decipher the book, you unlock a second code. This secondary code consists of the four steps that Sun Tzu teaches to advance a strategic position. Unlike the five factors, Sun Tzu never mentions these four steps directly, nor does he list them together. You must analyze the original Chinese, using the five factors to discover them. Together, the five factors and four steps decipher a deeper, clearer message in the text.

Your True Position

Before you can get where you are going, you must first know where you are. You use the five key factors to analyze your position and the positions of others. This strategic analysis is the topic of Sun Tzu's first chapter. These five factors are the "dimensions" that characterize a strategic position. These five dimensions are 1) your philosophy, 2) the changing climate, 3) the physical battleground, 4) your character, and 5) your abilities.

Your position is anchored by a core philosophy. Your philosophy defines your purpose or mission. A sense of purpose determines the way you see the world. Sun Tzu teaches that a warrior's philosophy unites him or her with others. Without a core philosophy that you share with others, you are isolated, alone, and strategically weak.

There are different levels of philosophy. Some philosophies are economic. People work with others only to get rewarded. Self-improvement is the basis for higher-level missions. Some individuals focus on developing their personal skills and knowledge. Many warriors work on this level. The most powerful philosophies are based on improving the world. In real war, people don't sacrifice their lives for money or self-improvement but because some ideals, such as freedom and democracy, are more important to them.

The next two dimensions of your strategic position describe your place in the world physically, in both time and space. Strategically, your environment has two opposite and yet complementary halves: the changing climate and the competitive ground. These two elements together mark your unique physical position. No one else can occupy the space you do at the same time.

Strategically, the changing climate is all the forces in nature and society that you cannot control. The weather and the seasons are natural examples of climate. The attitudes and beliefs of people around you are examples of the social climate. Though you cannot control climate, you can learn to use it to your advantage. Climate is controlled by time. The first rule of the climate is that it changes. A warrior does not fight against change. Instead, the warrior is trained to see change as the source of all opportunities.

The next dimension of your position is the ground where you choose to compete. This ground supports you and is the source of the rewards you seek. People compete in many different areas—in sports, in business, in academics, socially, in politics, and so on. Each provides a different form of support. The nature of that ground determines how you can advance your position. The ground is connected with the climate. When you choose a competitive arena, you also choose the climate associated with that ground.

Your personality and abilities also define your strategic position. Different people in similar physical circumstances have very different internal resources. Two opposite and complementary elements define your competitive potential: your character and your abilities.

Your character is the dimension of your strategic position that determines how well you make decisions. Sun Tzu calls this leadership. Warriors value five qualities—intelligence, courage, trustworthiness, discipline, and caring. These five character traits determine leadership ability. Warriors are not simply followers. To take the lead, you must have the intelligence and courage to make your own decisions. Others will trust you as a leader only if you demonstrate self-discipline and caring.

The last of the five factors defining your strategic position is ability, or what Sun Tzu calls methods. Ability comes from training. Sun Tzu defines strategy itself as an ability that results from training. While character is the realm of the individual, abilities or methods are the realm of group action. Your abilities define how well you work with others. Warriors realize that they cannot be successful in a vacuum. As Sun Tzu says, strategy depends on people, both understanding them and working with them.

These five factors together—your philosophy, the climate, the ground, your character, and your abilities—define your strategic position. They also determine how to advance a position over time.

Irresistible Force

Positions are not fixed in stone. Positions are dynamic. They are constantly changing. Time naturally erodes your position. If you do nothing to improve your situation, it will tend to get worse. Sun Tzu's first chapter is dedicated to analyzing your position. The next twelve chapters teach you how to defend and advance your position.

The four steps that strategy teaches to advance a position can overcome any obstacle. The strategic process creates an irresistible force. These four steps are 1) learning, 2) seeing, 3) moving, and 4) positioning. They represent a cycle, in which the last step of positioning leads to more learning, triggering another cycle of advance.

Each step in this cycle is intimately connected with the factors that define a strategic position. The basis of learning is the ground. Your competitive arena teaches you what you need to know. The basis of seeing is your character. Your individuality allows you to see certain opportunities. The basis of moving is the climate. The climate provides a window of opportunity for you to act. Finally, your abilities provide the basis of positioning. Your abilities allow you to defend and reap the rewards from your new position.

These four steps advance your position. For example, say you have a problem with someone at work or in your personal life. Sun Tzu teaches that the first step in transforming the situation is learning more about that person. As you learn more, you will see an opening, an opportunity to improve your relationship. For example, you might discover a common interest or a common enemy. Once you discover the opportunity, you have to act on it. That is, you have to change your position. Strategy teaches that you control the positions of others by shifting your own position, not by trying to move them directly. Finally, you have to evaluate whether or not your new position is more rewarding, and, if so, build on it.

These four steps create an endless cycle of improving your position. Learning more about your situation leads to seeing more opportunities. Seeing opportunities requires making decisions about whether to pursue them or not. Pursuing opportunities commits you to new positions that you must defend. These new positions become the launching point for a new cycle of advance.

Strategy teaches that small steps are the most powerful. Most of your advances should be small, quick, and seemingly minor. Over time, however, these little changes make a huge difference. You only need to make major changes in your position if you have made a major mistake. Small changes are much less risky and much more certain over time.

Invincible Strength

As you advance your position, you must maintain your strength. Sun Tzu defines strength as unity and focus, not size and power. Change naturally creates divisions among people, undermining unity. Change also makes it very difficult to maintain your focus. Both unity and focus arise from a shared philosophy and from an underlying concept we might call "oneness." Oneness means being complete or whole. Without this characteristic, you are alienated from those who are important to you. You get confused about the direction of your life.

On the group level, this oneness is the source of team unity. Unity is measured by how readily one member of a team relies on another. Warriors understand that a range of talent is more powerful than any single individual's talent. Without this underlying solidarity, teams are easily broken. Unity arises from the shared spirit that binds a team together, which is based on the core shared philosophy. Without shared goals, groups are quickly fragmented.

As you advance your position, philosophy makes up the stable core of your strategic position. As your position changes, the other four dimensions that define your strategic position evolve. The climate shifts. You win more ground. Your character develops. You learn more abilities. Amidst these changes, only your philosophy remains stable. Because of its stability, philosophy is the source of trust and faith that binds groups together.

A clear philosophy generates a different form of oneness on a personal level. It creates single-mindedness. When you have a clear mission or purpose, you never lose sight of your goal. You know what you want to achieve.

Another way to describe single-mindedness is focus. Regular people are not very successful because their focus wavers. They leave openings when their attention drifts. Warriors can spot and use those openings. Focus brings together all your resources at a specific time and place. This concentration of effort is the real source of power, according to the principles of strategy. This idea is familiar to anyone who has studied any physical martial art. In martial arts, the whole body concentrates on the point of attack.

Together, the oneness of unity and focus are the source of strength. In many ways, Sun Tzu wrote his work to counter the idea that strength comes from size, wealth, or even position. Most aspects of your position are external and temporary. Though the external dimensions of a position can contribute to your strength, it is your internal strength that matters in the long run.

How to Read This Book

Familiarity with the five key factors that define a position and the four steps that advance a position will help you understand the lessons of *The Art of War*. However, even with this basic understanding, much of the text is still hidden for the uninitiated.

For example, Sun Tzu often talks about "battle," "conflict," and "attack." In English, all these words are closely related, even interchangeable, but in *The Art of War*, these concepts are very different. "Attack" means moving into a new territory—sometimes to hamper another's advance, but not necessarily meeting an opponent. "Battle" means meeting an enemy or a challenge, but it doesn't necessarily mean conflict. "Conflict" is a destructive, hostile confrontation and the least desirable of the three actions.

Though we could spend a lot of time explaining how to decipher all the ideas in Sun Tzu's work (and we do in another book, *The Art of War Plus Its Amazing Secrets*), our goal in this work is to make it easy to use the magic of strategy in your life. To do this, we have decoded Sun Tzu's text in a very simple way.

The Warrior's Apprentice completes *The Art of War* so you can easily understand Sun Tzu's real meaning. We did not want to rewrite or obscure the original *The Art of War*, so we show a complete translation of Sun Tzu's original text on the left-hand pages. However, on the facing right-hand *Warrior's Apprentice* pages, we decode each line so you can use its ideas easily.

The simplest way to read this book is to read each line of *The Art of War,* followed by the parallel line in *The Warrior's Apprentice.* This deciphers the text so that even the uninitiated can use the magic of strategy easily.

In addition, we designed this book like a kaleidoscope so that it can be read in different ways to show different aspects of Sun Tzu's strategic principles. Reading one line at a time is the simplest, but when you read *The Art of War* one stanza or one page at a time, followed by the corresponding sections of *The Warrior's Apprentice*, you discover different shades of meaning.

As an introduction to the power of strategy, this book is the first step in developing the mind of a true warrior.

♦ ♦ ♦

"The path of the Warrior is lifelong, and mastery is often simply staying on the path."

In Search of the Warrior Spirit
Richard Strozzi-Heckler

Introduction

Five Elements and Nine Skills

Sun Tzu wrote his work based on the ancient tradition of Chinese science and philosophy. You will find his strategic magic much easier to use if you understand his five elements and nine skills based upon these ancient traditions.

Sun Tzu taught that success in competitive environments is not a matter of winning fights with others. Instead success depends on building and advancing strategic positions. *Positioning* is the core skill in his strategic system.

Sun Tzu taught that a general who fights a hundred battles and wins a hundred battles is not a good general. A good general is one who finds a position that wins without fighting a single battle. You win by building the right strategic positions and advancing those positions along the paths of least resistance.

Sun Tzu defines a position as based on *five elements*. These five elements—mission, climate, ground, the leader, and methods—define a strategic position and provide our basis for analyzing our positions relative to the positions of others. All the other skills of his toolkit for advancing positions—developing perspective, identifying opportunities, and so on—develop these elements.

The five elements defining positions are the underlying framework of Sun Tzu's work. However, Sun Tzu did not explain this system because his contemporaries understood it. Instead, his work was written to explain the differences between his elements and those of traditional Chinese science and their use in making strategic decisions.

To reach any goal, your job is decision-making. This is more than problem-solving. According to Sun Tzu, all problems are opportunities in disguise. If there were no problems, success would not require you to make decisions. However, you cannot be successful simply by tackling every problem. You must make decisions that advance your position. As you advance your strategic position, you solve most problems by leaving them behind. The solution to most problems is identifying the weakness in your position that creates them.

Sun Tzu taught that wars of attrition, that is, competitive battles where each competitor tries to tear down the other's position, cannot result in long-term success. This type of competition weaken both contesting parties, opening the way for outside competitors. To avoid wasting resources in such battles, Sun Tzu teaches you how to build positions that others cannot easily attack and ideally want to join.

Good strategy insists that you make the most of your strengths to compensate for your weaknesses. Your strengths and weaknesses do not come from your situation alone, but from your relative position within any group or organization. To make the right decisions, you must understand the key elements that define your strategic position.

Sun Tzu uses five elements to define your unique position within your competitive environment. These five elements—philosophy, heaven, ground, the leader, and methods—provide the backbone of a strategic approach to personal power. All the other parts in his system—primarily the nine skills for advancing a position,—flow from a good analysis of your management position based on these five factors.

The first element that defines a strategic position is what Sun Tzu called *philosophy* and we refer to as *mission*. A mission defines the goals and values at the core of a strategic position. To create success, this core philosophy must be shared. Every group has its own mission, and any organization serves a larger purpose. A clear idea of your mission within this larger purpose provides any group to which you belong with its unity and focus.

Sun Tzu also describes two internal characteristics: *uniting* and *focusing*. Though these concepts are separate in English, in Chinese they are closely connected. In Sun Tzu's system, both arise directly from your shared philosophy or mission. Uniting holds groups together. Focusing concentrates efforts in a single area. Both determine competitive strength. Strength is defined by the unity of a force, not its size.

Mission is the first element but it is the basis for the end point of advancing positions, *Winning Rewards*. In the end, every decision and action we make in our daily lives must lead to the winning rewards. Sun Tzu's system is fundamentally economic. You want to use the least time and effort to win the most possible rewards. This is not a matter of "selfishness" but of simply being effective. You alone can define the rewards that are important to you, but those rewards are most powerful when they are shared.

The next two factors define position within the larger environment. The importance of the environment is the great insight of Sun Tzu's work. He divides the environment into two opposite and yet complementary components, *climate(heaven)* and *ground (earth)*. Heaven and ground define the time and place of your position.

Sun Tzu taught that we view our environment too narrowly. His second key strategic skill defines specific techniques for *Developing Perspective* on our position in the environment so that we can see our position as others see us. A strategic position consists both of an objective reality and collection of subjective opinions about that reality. We can change objective reality only by first leveraging subjective opinions.

Climate arises from the forces of change. It is often translated as "heaven" or "weather" in the text. The cycle of the seasons is the most obvious changes in the natural environment, but every industry has its own business cycle and market climate. People's attitudes and emotions are key components of climate. This change erodes all existing positions and, at the same time, creates opportunities to advance your position. His third strategic skill uses change for *Identifying Opportunities* in the environment.

Ground is the economic foundation of your strategic position. It is both where you fight and what you fight for. In human society, the shape of the ground is defined by a network of relationships, which can be very different from the formal organizational chart. Unlike heaven, which is largely beyond our control, the ground that we control is determined by our own decisions. Choosing ground positions, moving to them, and utilizing them are the fourth strategic skill, *Leveraging Probability,* which teaches how different types of ground favors some types of positions over others.

Within the larger competitive environment, the unique characteristics of you and those with which you associate are also part of your strategic position. Sun Tzu breaks the important characteristics of a competitor into two opposite and complementary components: *the leader and methods.*

Decision-making is the unique responsibility of a *leader* in Sun Tzu's system. All people are, by definition, the leaders in their own lives because they make their own decisions. Leadership is the realm of individual action and character. You master Sun Tzu's strategy so that you can make the right decisions quickly.

A successful leader must make the right decisions quickly. This demands Sun Tzu's fifth and sixth key skills: *Minimizing Mistakes* and *Situation Response.* Minimizing mistakes focuses on a necessary economy of action, preserving our limited resources. Situation response teaches how to choose actions instantly based upon the key conditions of that define a situation.

Methods are the skills of working with others, the techniques of group organization. Our strategic success depends upon working with other people. Methods are the ways in which we interact with others. Generally, all of Sun Tzu's techniques can be described as methods. The literal translation of his book's title is "competitive methods."

Standard methods maintain existing processes. Good strategy requires innovating methods based on existing ones. Sun Tz's seventh skill is *Creating Momentum,* which requires combining standards with innovation. A leader's decisions must utilize and build on existing systems to make actions effective. You need a deep understanding of the working of the systems, skills, and organizations that affect your mission.

A rewarding position consists of the right combination of mission, climate, ground, leadership, and methods. Once we develop a rewarding position, others will try to take it from us. Defending positions is a necessary part of advancing them. It requires Sun Tzu's ninth and final skill, *Understanding Vulnerabilities.*

While Sun Tzu's work explains these nine skills for advancing positions, it does not take each skill in turn and explain it in detail. It does not offer examples as a contemporary work might. This is why we describe this work as an introduction to Sun Tzu's system as applied to the magic of Sun Tzu's strategy rather than as a complete description.

The Art of War was written to be concise. It starts with its most basic concepts, the five key elements, and then addresses progressively more complex and detailed ideas. Along the way, Sun Tzu tries to correct the most common misunderstandings and mistakes that people made in pursuing competitive success. In doing so, he uses analogies, metaphors, and historical references familiar to those of his time, but often lost on modern readers. We can adapt these references to the challenges of our personal lives but we cannot capture all of Sun Tzu's meaning.

If you are interested in a learning Sun Tzu's principles in more detail, we refer you to our on-line <u>Sun Tzu's Warrior's Rule Book</u>. This work details Sun Tzu's nine skill in terms of 232 interwoven principles. Each of these principles is explained as set of step-by-step rules. Each rule is illustrated by it application to a specific competitive challenge. Many of these challenges are drawn from modern management and business competition.

* * *

Chapter 1

Analysis: The Skill of Prophecy

The magic of strategy is that it gives you a framework for understanding the world and predicting the future. Since the world is complex and confusing, this first chapter gives you some simple tools to help you see what is coming. Instead of running away from apparent problems or getting into unnecessary fights with people, warriors must make no assumptions about their position in the world. The skill of prophecy comes from careful analysis.

In his first chapter, Sun Tzu divides the warrior's world into five key components. You use this framework to understand your position in the world and your possibilities.

Sun Tzu then divides society into two types of people. There are warriors, who constantly question their situation. Then there are regular people, who simply never question their assumptions. Warriors open themselves up to outside viewpoints. They listen to others. They ask for help. They work to get to the truth.

Warriors know that they cannot simply trust words or even actions at face value. Appearances are deceptive. Everyone controls how he or she looks to others. To be a warrior, you must learn to see through the illusions of the world.

Strategic analysis comes down to gathering verifiable facts and putting them together logically. Our desires and fears mislead us. Instead of acting out of emotion, we must learn analysis so we can understand where we can succeed.

Analysis

NOTE: *You can read this book horizontally or vertically.*

SUN TZU SAID:

This is war. 1

It is the most important skill in the nation.
It is the basis of life and death.
It is the philosophy of survival or destruction.
You must know it well.

6Your skill comes from five factors.
Study these factors when you plan war.
You must insist on knowing your situation.
1. Discuss philosophy.
2. Discuss the climate.
3. Discuss the ground.
4. Discuss leadership.
5. Discuss military methods.

14It starts with your military philosophy.
Command your people in a way that gives
them a higher shared purpose.
You can lead others to death.
You can lead others to life.
They must never fear danger or dishonesty.

DEFINITIONS:

*As in a work of
mathematics,
Sun Tzu starts
by defining his
terms precisely
and using them
consistently
throughout.*

The Skill of Prophecy

NOTE: *Read a line across both pages at once or down each page separately.*

A WARRIOR HEARS:

1 This is the warrior's way.
You must master the skills of meeting challenges.
These skills are the difference between feeling alive and feeling dead.
These skills are the difference between success and failure.
You must master the magic of strategy.

Your strategic position is defined by five characteristics.
Focus on these five aspects when you face a challenge.
Ask these questions to understand your position.

1. What is your purpose?
2. How is your situation changing?
3. Where can you make progress?
4. What is your character?
5. What abilities do you have?

POSITION:

It starts with your life's purpose.
You can win respect from others only on the basis of sharing their goals and ideals.
Some values are worth dying for.
Some values make life worth living.
Values protect you from threats and deception.

These five factors define a "competitive position" and provide a framework for categorizing all relevant facts.

¹⁹Next, you have the climate.
It can be sunny or overcast.
It can be hot or cold.
It includes the timing of the seasons.

²³Next is the terrain.
It can be distant or near.
It can be difficult or easy.
It can be open or narrow.
It also determines your life or death.

²⁸Next is the commander.
He must be smart, trustworthy, caring, brave, and strict.

³⁰Finally, you have your military methods.
They include the shape of your organization.
They come from your management philosophy.
You must master their use.

CHARACTERS:

Chinese characters are concepts, not verbs, nouns, or other parts of speech. For example, the character 軍 *means* **make war**, **army**, *and* **military**.

³⁴All five of these factors are critical.
As a commander, you must pay attention to them.
Understanding them brings victory.
Ignoring them means defeat.

You must see how your world is changing.
Your future can temporarily look bright or dismal.
Your luck will temporarily run hot and cold.
However, everything changes in cycles of time.

You must know how to pick your battles.
You can choose long-term or short-term goals.
Your choices determine how hard or easy your life is.
You can choose broad or specific targets.
Picking the right battles also determines your success or failure.

Next, you must accept responsibility.
Be wise, dependable, sensitive, courageous, and disciplined.

Finally, you need to develop specific abilities and talents.
These skills determine how well you work with others.
Your skills arise from what you really believe is important in life.
You need to train yourself to be successful.

Every one of these five facts is important to your success.
They are what create your opportunities.
If you accept your situation, you will be successful.
If you deny your situation, you will be a failure.

KNOWLEDGE:

Sun Tzu taught that competitive success is based on your use of knowledge rather than on size, strength, or wealth.

You must learn through planning. 2
You must question the situation.

[3]You must ask:
Which government has the right philosophy?
Which commander has the skill?
Which season and place has the advantage?
Which method of command works?
Which group of forces has the strength?
Which officers and men have the training?
Which rewards and punishments make sense?
This tells when you will win and when you will lose.

Some commanders perform this analysis.
If you use these commanders, you will win.
Keep them.
Some commanders ignore this analysis.
If you use these commanders, you will lose.
Get rid of them.

FORMULAS

Each Chinese phrase is more like a mathematical formula than an English sentence, a precise statement of relationships.

Plan an advantage by listening. 3
Adjust to the situation.
Get assistance from the outside.
Influence events.
Then planning can find opportunities and
give you control.

2 Warriors learn from strategic analysis.
You must question your assumptions.

You must always be wondering:
Which group has the most powerful philosophy?
How good am I at making decisions?
When and where are my best opportunities?
How well do I communicate with others?
What groups of people will support me?
What leaders and companions can I learn from?
What rewards are worth the risks?
This simple analysis tells you if you are headed for success or failure.

Warriors are those who are willing to question their position.
If you spend your time with these warriors, you will be successful.
Stay with them.
Ordinary people are unwilling to question their position.
If you follow the mindless crowd, you will fail.
Avoid the thoughtless.

3 Warriors discover opportunities by listening.
Act on reality, not your limited perceptions.
Seek help from those with a broader viewpoint.
Control what happens in your life.
This is how you discover your options and create your future.

RELATIVITY:

The strength or weakness of a position depends on how it compares to other positions around it, which you learn by listening.

Warfare is one thing. 4
It is a philosophy of deception.

³When you are ready, you try to appear incapacitated.
When active, you pretend inactivity.
When you are close to the enemy, you appear distant.
When far away, you pretend you are near.

⁷You can have an advantage and still entice an opponent.
You can be disorganized and still be decisive.
You can be ready and still be preparing.
You can be strong and still avoid battle.
You can be angry and still stop yourself.
You can humble yourself and still be confident.
You can be relaxed and still be working.
You can be close to an ally and still part ways.
You can attack a place without planning to do so.
You can leave a place without giving away your plan.

RESPONSES

Because no one knows your position as well as you do, your position is partly defined by your own re- actions to your situation.

¹⁷You will find a place where you can win.
You cannot first signal your intentions.

4 A warrior's way is one thing.
It is the path through the world's illusions.

People will act confident when they are insecure.
People can seem lazy when they are struggling.
People can pretend to be concerned when they are uncaring.
People can appear indifferent when they are worried.

When people tempt you, you must suspect their motives.
Apparently clear-thinking people can be confused.
Seemingly well-equipped people can be poorly prepared.
Those who avoid a fight can be very strong.
Those who appear indifferent can be very emotional.
Those who feign self-assurance can be frightened.
People can work very hard to appear easygoing.
People can be good friends but compete with one another.
People can use opportunities without creating them.
Your direction is not determined by where you come from.

The world offers you plenty of opportunities.
You must be careful of the messages you send.

DECEPTION:

If information is the basis of success, you must factor in deception to evaluate and control the flow of information in competition.

Manage to avoid battle until your organization can count 5 on certain victory.
You must calculate many advantages.
Before you go to battle, your organization's analysis can indicate that you may not win.
You can count few advantages.
Many advantages add up to victory.
Few advantages add up to defeat.
How can you know your advantages without analyzing them?
We can see where we are by means of our observations.
We can foresee our victory or defeat by planning.

BATTLE:

Sun Tzu's terms are precise. For example, the character 戰 is translated as **battle,** *but it means engaging an enemy or meeting a challenge, not violent conflict.*

5 Warriors are patient enough to wait until the odds are all in their favor.

You must choose a path that offers many opportunities.

If your success is uncertain, prior analysis of the five factors will predict the problem.

You must avoid paths that offer few opportunities.

Paths with many opportunities lead to success.

Paths with few opportunities lead to failure.

How can you see your path objectively without doing the work?

Warriors train themselves to see their situation as it truly is.

This is how the skill of prophecy creates success and prevents failure.

CHALLENGES:

You do not "battle" or challenge opponents until you are certain your position can dominate their position, not just in one category, but in many different ones.

Related Articles from *Sun Tzu's Playbook*

In this first chapter, Sun Tzu introduces the basics of positioning. We explore these ideas in more detail in our Sun Tzu's Art of War Playbook. *To learn the step-by-step techniques for positioning, we recommend the* Playbook *articles listed below.*

1.0.0 Strategic Positioning: developing relatively superior positions.

1.1.0 Position Paths: the continuity of strategic positions over time.

1.1.1 Position Dynamics: how all current positions evolve over time.

1.1.2 Defending Positions: defending current positions until new positions are established.

1.2 Subobjective Positions: the subjective and objective aspects of a position.

1.2.1 Competitive Landscapes: the arenas in which rivals jockey for position.

1.2.2 Exploiting Exploration: how competitive landscapes are searched and positions identified.

1.2.3 Position Complexity: how positions arise from interactions in complex environments.

1.3 Elemental Analysis: the relevant components of all competitive positions.

1.3.1 Competitive Comparison: competition as the comparison of positions.

1.3.2 Element Scalability: how elements of a position scale up to larger positions.

1.4 The External Environment: external conditions shaping strategic positions.

1.4.1 Climate Shift: forces of environmental change shaping temporary conditions.

1.4.2 Ground Features: the persistent resources that we can control.

1.5 Competing Agents: the key characteristics of competitors.

1.5.1 Command Leadership: individual decision-making.

1.5.2. Group Methods: systems for executing decisions.

1.6 Mission Values: the goals and values needed for motivation.

1.6.1 Shared Mission: finding goals that others can share.

1.6.2 Types of Motivations: hierarchies of motivation that define missions.

1.6.3 Shifting Priorities: how missions change according to temporary conditions.

Chapter 2

Going to War: The Choice of Paths

In his second chapter, Sun Tzu teaches you about price of failure. When you seek to advance your position in a challenging world, your actions cost time and energy. These resources are limited. The magic of strategy is that it enables you, by making the right choices, to avoid wasting time and energy.

This chapter begins by discussing the price of failure. The warrior's way is not painless. Warriors realize that every choice they make has a cost attached to it. Regular people are blissfully unaware of the costs of their decisions. As a warrior's apprentice, you must learn to appreciate the harsh reality of unavoidable costs in the face of limited resources.

Sun Tzu's strategy balances costs with potential rewards. Sun Tzu teaches an economics of conservation. A warrior learns to evaluate every potential move based on its investment in size, time, and space. The bigger, more time-consuming, and more distant an opportunity is, the most costly and risky it is. For this reason, Sun Tzu teaches you to move forward in small, quick, local advances. Small steps are more powerful because they are less risky.

The second part of choosing the right path is identifying opportunities that return more than they consume. Some paths can save you effort, time, and distance. You can identify and put your efforts into activities that increase your capabilities and resources over time. Warriors invest today in efforts that make them more powerful tomorrow.

Going to War

SUN TZU SAID:

Everything depends on your use of military philosophy. 1
Moving the army requires thousands of vehicles.
These vehicles must be loaded thousands of times.
The army must carry a huge supply of arms.
You need ten thousand acres of grain.
This results in internal and external shortages.
Any army consumes resources like an invader.
An army uses up glue and paint for wood.
An army requires armor for its vehicles.
People complain about the waste of a vast amount of metal.
It will set you back when you attempt to raise tens of thousands of troops.

12Using a huge army makes war very expensive to win.
Long delays create a dull army and sharp defeats.
Attacking enemy cities drains your forces.

KNOWLEDGE:

The charac-ter 知 *means* knowledge, *and it illustrates* **a person** 矢 *next to* **a mouth** 口.
This forms a picture of listening.

The Choice of Paths

THE WARRIOR HEARS:

1 Warriors change everything by the choices they make.
You move forward choosing among thousands of possibilities.
You make thousands of choices about which paths to take.
Your choices can require tremendous amounts of time and effort.
You need enough resources to satisfy your needs.
Your mental and physical assets are limited.
Any endeavor can demand more than it is worth.
Building positions requires connections and art.
Your position requires protection to advance.
People complain that building positions costs too much time and effort.
Still, you will only lose ground if you try to become successful becoming popular or famous.

MINIMIZE:

Each line here is a separate rule for minimizing the risks of competition. They are in a highly condensed form
.

Size is the first form of cost that makes success more unlikely.
Large projects require preparation that slows your progress.
Setting oversized goals just saps your energy.

Long violent campaigns that exhaust the nation's resources
are wrong.

[16]You can control a dull army.
You will suffer sharp defeats.
You can drain your forces.
Your money will be used up.
Your rivals will multiply as your army collapses, and they will
begin against you.
It doesn't matter how smart you are.
You cannot get ahead by taking losses!

[23]You hear of people going to war too quickly.
Still, you won't see a skilled war that lasts a long time.

[25]You can fight a war for a long time or you can make your
nation strong.
You can't do both.

Make no assumptions about all the 2
dangers in using military force.
Then you won't make assumptions about the
benefits of using arms either.

[3]You want to make good use of war.
Do not raise troops repeatedly.
Do not carry too many supplies.
Choose to be useful to your nation.
Feed off the enemy.
Make your army carry only the provisions it needs.

KNOWLEDGE:

The Chinese 知
means knowl-
edge, *and it*
illustrates **a**
person 矢 *next to*
a **mouth** 口.
This forms a
picture of listen-
ing.

Conflicts that consume your limited time and resources lead only to your failure.

Oversized goals lead to stagnation.
The larger your failure, the more painful it is.
You can expend all your reserves.
Your can overstretch your resources.
This just creates a whole new set of problems, stopping your progress and inviting disaster.
You must avoid getting in over your head.
You cannot succeed by risking everything.

You can jump at an opportunity without enough preparation.
But large investments of time are always costly to your success.

You can invest in long, drawn-out campaigns or you can advance with quick moves forward.
Wasting time makes steady progress impossible.

2 Warriors never pretend that they know all the risks in choosing a course of action.
Because you cannot know all the costs in advance, you cannot know your eventual rewards either.

You must invest your efforts wisely.
Do not repeat you mistakes.
Plan to use small steps forward.
Put your efforts into improving your productivity.
Feed of f of challenges.
Do not carry any baggage you don't need.

MINIMIZE:

Each line here is a separate rule for minimizing the risks of competition. Like all of Sun Tzu's work, they are in a highly condensed form .

The nation impoverishes itself shipping to troops that 3 are far away.

Distant transportation is costly for hundreds of families.

Buying goods with the army nearby is also expensive.

High prices also exhaust wealth.

If you exhaust your wealth, you then quickly hollow out your military.

Military forces consume a nation's wealth entirely.

War leaves households in the former heart of the nation with nothing.

[8]War destroys hundreds of families.

Out of every ten families, war leaves only seven.

War empties the government's storehouses.

Broken armies will get rid of their horses.

They will throw down their armor, helmets, and arrows.

They will lose their swords and shields.

They will leave their wagons without oxen.

War will consume 60 percent of everything you have.

Because of this, it is the intelligent commander's duty to 4 feed off the enemy.

[2]Use a cup of the enemy's food.

It is worth twenty of your own.

Win a bushel of the enemy's feed.

It is worth twenty of your own.

3 Warriors who move too far from what they know find that they are poorer for it.

Distance is another form of cost that makes success unlikely.

The further you go, the higher the price you must pay.

You cannot afford the cost of far-flung projects.

The efforts you put into traveling cannot also be used to build up your position.

Moving too far afield can destroy your position completely.

Long-distance campaigns erode dependable forms of support and erode your position.

The life of the warrior is inherently dangerous.

Many attempts at advancing your position are doomed to fail.

Every attempt at moving forward is costly.

Don't risk your future mobility on the possibility of failure.

You must maintain sources of support to defend your position.

Warriors always know how to hold onto their assets.

Warriors always protect their ability to move.

Warriors keep advances small, quick, and local to minimize costs.

4 Warriors maintain their resources through campaigns that return more than they consume.

You can win more time.

An hour spent today can save twenty hours in the future.

You can leverage your finances.

Invest a dollar today to save twenty dollars in the future.

[6]You can kill the enemy and frustrate him as well.
Take the enemy's strength from him by stealing away his
money.

[8]Fight for the enemy's supply wagons.
Capture his supplies by using overwhelming force.
Reward the first who capture them.
Then change their banners and flags.
Mix them in with your own wagons to increase your supply
line.
Keep your soldiers strong by providing for them.
This is what it means to beat the enemy while you grow
more powerful.

Make victory in war pay for itself. 5
Avoid expensive, long campaigns.
The military commander's knowledge is the key.
Knowledge determines if the civilian officials can govern.
Knowledge determines if the nation's households
are peaceful or a danger to the state.

PEACE:

The character for **peace** 安 *shows a woman under a roof requiring protection.*

You can improve your situation and gain resources as well.
Address the difficulties that steal away your resources and weaken your position.

Put your energy into challenges that win you more resources.
Win financial and others support by obviously doing good work.
When people give you support, you must always reward them.
You must make each channel of support and income your own.
You want to get your friends and family involved to solidify your sources of income.
Keep yourself strong by having independent means.
Warriors advance their positions in ways that give them more resources to draw upon.

5 Warriors recognize progress by how it increases their abilities.
Make the least costly choices to move toward your goals.
The key to cost control is having the right information.
You must know how to support yourself to control your life.
Information is what allows you to reap the rewards of progress and avoid the costs of conflict.

◆ ◆ ◆

VICTORY:

Our book **The Warrior Class** *expands each stanza of the text into a strategy lesson.*

Related Articles from *Sun Tzu's Playbook*

In his second chapter, Sun Tzu teaches basic competitive economics. We explore these ideas in more detail in our **Sun Tzu's Art of War Playbook***. To learn the step-by-step techniques for economical political campaigning, we recommend the articles listed below.*

1.3.1 Competitive Comparison: competition as the comparison of positions.

1.6.1 Shared Mission: finding goals that others can share.

1.8.3 Cycle Time: speed in feedback and reaction.

1.8.4 Probabilistic Process: the role of chance in strategic processes and systems.

2.2.1 Personal Relationships: how information depends on personal relationships.

2.2.2 Mental Models: how mental models simplify decision-making.

2.3.4 Using Questions: using questions in gathering information and predicting reactions.

3.1 Strategic Economics: balancing the cost and benefits of positioning.

3.1.1 Resource Limitations: the inherent limitation of strategic resources.

3.1.2 Strategic Profitability: understanding gains and losses.

3.1.3 Conflict Cost: the costly nature of resolving competitive comparisons by conflict.

3.1.4 Openings: seeking openings to avoid costly conflict.

3.1.5 Unpredictable Value: the limitations of predicting the value of positions.

3.1.6 Time Limitations: the time limits on opportunities.

4.0 Leveraging Probability: better decisions regarding our choice of opportunities.

4.1 Future Potential: the limitations and potential of current and future positions.

4.2 Choosing Non-Action: choosing between action and non-action.

5.3 Reaction Time: the use of speed in choosing actions.

5.3.1 Speed and Quickness: the use of pace within a dynamic environment.

5.3.2 Opportunity Windows: the effect of speed upon opposition.

5.3.3 Information Freshness: choosing actions based on freshness of information.

5.4 Minimizing Action: minimizing waste, i.e., less is more.

5.4.1 Testing Value : choosing actions to test for value.

5.4.2 Successful Mistakes: learning from our mistakes.

5.5 Focused Power: size consideration in safe experimentation.

5.5.1 Force Size: limiting the size of force in an advance.

5.5.2 Distance Limitations: the use of short steps to reach distant goals.

Chapter 3

Planning an Attack: The Power of Fellowship

Warriors realize that their success always depends on other people. The magic of strategy requires an understanding of human psychology, especially how people act in groups. For Sun Tzu, group psychology is closely tied to philosophy because a shared philosophy is what binds groups together.

In this chapter's first section, Sun Tzu discusses how unity creates success. The goal of unity—and focusing on the tasks at hand—is not to win confrontations but to develop positions that others do not want to attack.

Sun Tzu lists the ways that you can deal with groups of opponents. Sun Tzu lists these measures in the order of their effectiveness. He warns against the worst way of dealing with rivals: attacking them when they are concentrated in a large group.

Strategy teaches the strategic approach to success in the face of opposition: using small, focused engagements in which your group has a clear advantage. He explains how the relative size of competing groups determines the type of engagements you want to create.

The topic then changes to how political divisions undermine the strength of a group. A divided group loses its focus and the result is disastrous. All groups need clear leaders.

Group leaders need certain types of knowledge and skill to make good decisions. You must join groups with good leadership. Leaders are judged by how well they know their teammates, their opponents, their competitive area, and the trends of the climate.

Planning an Attack

SUN TZU SAID:

Everyone relies on the arts of war. 1
A united nation is strong.
A divided nation is weak.
A united army is strong.
A divided army is weak.
A united force is strong.
A divided force is weak.
United men are strong.
Divided men are weak.
A united unit is strong.
A divided unit is weak.

OPPOSITES:

Most of Sun Tzu's concepts are defined as complementary opposites, such as **complete** *(united)* 全 *and* **broken** *(divided)* 破.

[12]Unity works because it enables you to win every battle you fight.
Still, this is the foolish goal of a weak leader.
Avoid battle and make the enemy's men surrender.
This is the right goal for a superior leader.

The best way to make war is to ruin the enemy's plans. 2
The next best is to disrupt alliances.
The next best is to attack the opposing army.
The worst is to attack the enemy's cities.

The Power of Fellowship

THE WARRIOR HEARS:

1 We all understand the power of teamwork.
As part of united team, you are stronger.
A group that is divided makes you weaker.
A unified team is focused on its external goals.
A divided group focuses on internal differences.
A united team has momentum.
A divided group gets stuck.
People can use their unique talents in a team.
People must do everything themselves alone.
Every individual is known on a team.
Every individual is faceless in a crowd .

STRENGTH:

*The key element discussed here is **philosophy**, which is the basis of **unity** and **focus**, which are the basis for strength.*

Regular people join teams because teams can
consistently surpass individuals.
This is not a worthy goal for a warrior.
Warriors seek to win individuals over to their team.
This is the best focus for the best decisions.

2 Warriors undermine opposition by acting before opponents do.
You can divide opponents by leveraging philosophical differences.
Your group should move against opposing groups only when necessary.
You must never move against an opponent's established position.

5This is what happens when you attack a city.
You can attempt it, but you can't finish it.
First you must make siege engines.
You need the right equipment and machinery.
It takes three months and still you cannot win.
Then you try to encircle the area.
You use three more months without making progress.
Your command still doesn't succeed and this angers you.
You then try to swarm the city.
This kills a third of your officers and men.
You are still unable to draw the enemy out of the city.
This attack is a disaster.

Make good use of war. 3
Make the enemy's troops surrender.
You can do this fighting only minor battles.
You can draw the enemy's men out of their cities.
You can do it with small attacks.
You can destroy the men of a nation.
You must keep your campaign short.

ATTACK:

The character
attack 知 *means*
moving into
new territory.
It is different
from **conflict**
争, *which is a*
violent
confrontation.

8You must use total war, fighting with every-
thing you have.
Never stop fighting when at war.
You can gain complete advantage.
To do this, you must plan your strategy of
attack.

Opposing groups in a superior position leads to failure.

It is tempting to fight others for choice positions but it never works.

You think you can undermine the strength of their position.

This requires a huge investment of your limited resources.

This futile effort is doomed to waste your time and resources.

You can try to get around a superior position.

You waste more of your time in an effort that gets you nowhere.

You are naturally frustrated, and you are consumed by hostility.

You eventually lash out in rage.

This foolishness costs you many of your supporters and friends.

You cannot displace the opposing groups from their position.

Fighting against established positions is a tragedy.

3 Warriors use their strategic position.

You must know how to win away an opposing group's support.

You do this by advancing your position one small step at a time.

You can lure a group's members away from their position.

You must understand the power of focused attacks.

Over time, your progress can undermine the largest opponents.

You do this a little at a time.

You always work to advance your position, using every opportunity.

It is your persistence that brings you success.

You can overcome any challenge you face.

Your success depends entirely on choosing methods that work.

MINIMIZE:

Since you cannot control the results of a plan, the first rule is to control what you can, which is how much you invest.

¹²The rules for making war are:
If you outnumber enemy forces ten to one, surround them.
If you outnumber them five to one, attack them.
If you outnumber them two to one, divide them.
If you are equal, then find an advantageous battle.
If you are fewer, defend against them.
If you are much weaker, evade them.

¹⁹Small forces are not powerful.
However, large forces cannot catch them.

You must master command. 4
The nation must support you.

³Supporting the military makes the nation powerful.
Not supporting the military makes the nation weak.

⁵The army's position is made more difficult by politicians in
three different ways.
Ignorant of a military division's inability to advance, they
order an advance.
Ignorant of a military division's inability to withdraw, they
order a withdrawal.
We call this tying up the army.
They don't understands a military division's function.
Still, they think they can govern military divisions.
This confuses the army's officers.

The rules for making choices are.
Overwhelming size wins by engulfing challenges.
Dominant size wins by challenging opponents.
Superior size wins by dividing opponents.
Equal size wins by picking challenges that opponents cannot meet.
Smaller size wins by defending well-protected positions.
Insignificant size wins by staying ahead of opponents.

Large groups of people have the advantage of power.
Small groups of people have the advantage of speed.

4 Warriors know how to lead a group.
You must know how to win the support of your companions.

Having the support of others makes you powerful.
Not having the support of others makes you weak.

If you are part of a team in which competing interests influence
decision-making, you must expect certain problems.
Divided groups often act to benefit a part of the group while hurt-
ing the organization as a whole.
Divided groups often act to protect some members to the detriment
of other members.
Internal politics divides many groups.
Politicians destroy every group's focus on its mission.
Politicians have their own agendas.
Politicians make decision-making difficult.

¹²Politicians don't know the military division of authority.
They think all military divisions are the same.
This will create distrust among the army's officers.

¹⁵Military divisions can become confused and suspicious.
This invites invasion by many different rivals.
We say correctly that disorder in an army kills victory.

You must know five things to win: 5
Victory comes from knowing when to attack and when to avoid battle.
Victory comes from correctly using both large and small forces.
Victory comes from everyone sharing the same goals.
Victory comes from finding opportunities in problems.
Victory comes from having a capable commander and the government leaving him alone.
You must know these five things.
You then know the theory of victory.

We say: 6
"Know yourself and know your enemy.
You will be safe in every battle.
You may know yourself but not know the enemy.
You will then lose one battle for every one you win.
You may not know yourself or the enemy.
You will then lose every battle."

IGNORANCE:

Many opposites consist of a character, for example, **know** 知, *and the negated character,* **not** 不 **know** 知, *for ignorance.*

Internal politics confuses a group's priorities.
Without clear priorities, any decision can be defended.
Leaders in a group must have confidence in one another.

A breakdown in a group's unity and focus creates weakness.
Weakness in an organization invites attack.
Without solid leadership, no group can be successful.

5 Warriors focus on five things to succeed.
You must know when to your get into something new and when it
is best to avoid taking on new challenges.
You must know how to judge the relative size of the commitments
you make.
You must join teams who share your goals and philosophy.
You must discover opportunities by facing your biggest fears.
You must recognize that you must make your own
decisions and wait for someone else to direct you.
You must take responsibility for these five things.
You then know how to make good choices.

6 Warriors hear:
You must know yourself and your challenges.
You can then safely meet every challenge.
You can know yourself but not understand the
challenge.
Then, for every success you have, you will have a
setback.
If you misjudge yourself and or your challenges.
You will fail at everything.

MAPPING:

*Most concepts
such as the "five
victories" above
map to other as-
pects of the Sun
Tzu's system, in
this case the five
key elements.*

Related Articles from *Sun Tzu's Playbook*

In this third chapter, Sun Tzu introduces the basics of advancing into new areas. To learn the step-by-step techniques involved, we recommend the Sun Tzu's Art of War Playbook *articles listed below.*

1.1.1 Position Dynamics: how all current positions are always getting better or worse.

1.1.2 Defending Positions: how we defend our current positions until new positions are established.

1.2 Subobjective Positions: the subjective and objective aspects of a position.

1.3.1 Competitive Comparison: competition as the comparison of positions.

1.7 Competitive Power: the sources of superiority in challenges.

1.7.1 Team Unity: strength by joining with others.

1.7.2 Goal Focus: strength as arising from concentrating efforts.

1.8 Progress Cycle: the adaptive loop by which positions are advanced.

1.8.1 Creation and Destruction: the creation and destruction of competitive positions.

1.8.2 The Adaptive Loop: the continual reiteration of position analysis.

2.3.6 Promises and Threats: the use of promises and threats as strategic moves.

2.4 Contact Networks: the range of contacts needed to create perspective.

2.4.1 Ground Perspective: getting information on a new competitive arena.

2.4.2 Climate Perspective: getting perspective on temporary external conditions.

3.0.0 Identifying Opportunities: the use of opportunities to advance a position.

3.1.3 Conflict Cost: the costly nature of resolving competitive comparisons by conflict.

3.2 Opportunity Creation: how change creates opportunities.

3.2.2 Opportunity Invisibility: why opportunities are always hidden.

3.2.4 Emptiness and Fullness: the transformations between strength and weakness.

3.4 Dis-Economies of Scale: how opportunities are created by the size of others.

3.4.2 Opportunity Fit: finding new opportunities that fit your size.

3.4.3 Reaction Lag: how size creates temporary openings.

3.5 Strength and Weakness: openings created by the strength of others.

3.6 Leveraging Subjectivity: openings between subjective and objective positions.

3.7 Defining the Ground: redefining a competitive arena to create relative mismatches.

5.6 Defensive Advances: balancing defending and advancing positions.

Chapter 4

Positioning: The Place of Judgment

We could call strategy the lazy person's path to success. The whole purpose of strategy is to find easy ways to achieve your goals and the easiest places that allow you to pursue them.

Real warriors, unlike make-believe warriors, don't go looking for big fights. They don't feel the need to prove to anyone how smart or brave they are. They certainly don't need to do stupid or dangerous things to create the appearance of courage. Warriors don't care about image. They care about what is real.

You make success easy by using your existing position as your springboard to future success. Regular people tend to think negatively about their current situation. This negativity results in a sense of inadequacy and inferiority. Warriors see the unique value in their position. Warriors are keenly aware of their own assets.

If you value your existing position, you will do what you must to protect it. Regular people take their situation for granted. They neglect maintaining what they have. The result is that their situation always tends to get worse. Warriors prize their existing position and defend it fiercely. They realize that their current situation is the core of all their future success.

Without a proper appreciation for what you already have, you cannot move forward. Regular people envy other people's positions and their opportunities. Warriors see that their positions offer the best possible opportunities for them. You can duplicate the methods of others, but you must find your own path.

Positioning

Learn from the history of successful battles. **1**
Your first actions should deny victory to the enemy.
You pay attention to your enemy to find the way to win.
You alone can deny victory to the enemy.
Only your enemy can allow you to win.

[6]You must fight well.
You can prevent the enemy's victory.
You cannot win unless the enemy enables your
victory.

[9]We say:
You see the opportunity for victory; you don't
create it.

ENEMY

In Sun Tzu's system, the **enemy** 敵 *is defined as the other actors in the environment that create opportunities for success.*

You are sometimes unable to win. **2**
You must then defend.
You will eventually be able to win.
You must then attack.
Defend when you have insufficient strength.
Attack when you have a surplus of strength.

The Place of Judgment

1 Observe successful people and copy them.
Your first duty is to protect your existing position.
Study openings that others leave to see your opportunities.
Do not give anyone an opening to attack you.
Wait until others offer you an opening as a path to your success.

Use your efforts wisely.
What you do determines how safe you are.
What other people do determines where your opportunities lie.

Warriors learn.
Open your eyes to see the opportunities that are available to you.

POSITION:

The theme of this chapter is using your position, specifically your position on the **ground***, which must be defensible.*

2 You must be patient when frustrated.
Protect what you already have.
Time opens up new opportunities.
Take advantage of them without hesitation.
Build up your abilities when you lack skills.
Move into new areas when you have the resources.

7You must defend yourself well.
Save your forces and dig in.
You must attack well.
Move your forces when you have a clear advantage.

11You must always protect yourself until you can completely
triumph.

Some may see how to win. 3
However, they cannot position their forces where they must.
This demonstrates limited ability.

4Some can struggle to a victory and the whole world may
praise their winning.
This also demonstrates a limited ability.

6Win as easily as picking up a fallen hair.
Don't use all of your forces.
See the time to move.
Don't try to find something clever.
Hear the clap of thunder.
Don't try to hear something subtle.

12Learn from the history of successful battles.
Victory goes to those who make winning easy.
A good battle is one that you will obviously win.
It doesn't take intelligence to win a reputation.
It doesn't take courage to achieve success.

Always protect your position.
Conserve your resources and keep a low profile.
Always look for opportunities to advance your position.
Wait to move until you know that you can move successfully.

Avoid risking your existing position until you are certain that you can move forward.

3 Some people find it easy to see opportunities.
These people, however, often lack the courage to make a move.
Vision without action gets you nowhere.

Others make the mistake of fighting costly battles that they need luck to win.
Action without judgment also gets you nowhere.

Good strategy teaches you to take small steps forward.
Keep some resources in reserve just in case.
Wait until you have a clear opening.
Don't imagine opportunities where none exist.
Real opportunities are always clear-cut.
Imaginary opportunities are always elusive.

The most lasting progress requires picking the right opportunities.
Warriors are not heroes who look for difficult challenges.
A challenge is worthwhile if it moves you forward easily.
People who fight battles to build a reputation are foolish.
Only fools look for glory at the expense of success.

¹⁷You must win your battles without effort.

Avoid difficult struggles.

Fight when your position must win.

You always win by preventing your defeat.

²¹You must engage only in winning battles.

Position yourself where you cannot lose.

Never waste an opportunity to defeat your enemy.

²⁴You win a war by first assuring yourself of victory.

Only afterward do you look for a fight.

Outmaneuver the enemy before the first battle and then

fight to win.

You must make good use of war. 4

Study military philosophy and the art of defense.

You can control your victory or defeat.

⁴This is the art of war:

"1. Discuss the distances.

2. Discuss your numbers.

3. Discuss your calculations.

4. Discuss your decisions.

5. Discuss victory.

LEVERAGE:

What we call **leverage** *is described by the characters* **no** 不 **excess** 弍 *and comes from correctly as utilizing your* **position** 措.

¹⁰The ground determines the distance.

The distance determines your numbers.

Your numbers determine your calculations.

Your calculations determine your decisions.

Your decisions determine your victory."

Strategy is the lazy person's path to success.
Avoid the hard work.
Let your position work for you.
You must never leave openings that others can attack.

Warriors avoid fights they cannot win.
Warriors avoid positions they cannot defend.
You must use every opportunity that comes your way.

Success over the long term requires developing your position.
Choose stepping-stones that make the next step forward easy.
You gradually advance your position to make capturing your next objective easy.

4 You must make good use of comparing opportunities.
You must know what values are worth defending.
Your choices determine what happens to you.

This is how you choose the best opportunities.
1. Keep close to what you already know.
2. Count if you have enough time and resources.
3. Balance the positive and negative odds.
4. Select the path that offers the easiest choices.
5. Choose the clearest definition of success.

EASE:

At this point, you have read over a hundred competitive rules. The easiest way to remember them is to learn their connections.

Your current position generates your knowledge.
Your knowledge creates your time and resources.
Your resources determine odds of success.
The odds determine how easy your choices will be.
Your choices must lead to a clear sense of success .

[15]Creating a winning war is like balancing a coin of gold
against a coin of silver.
Creating a losing war is like balancing a coin of silver
against a coin of gold.

Winning a battle is always a matter of people.
You pour them into battle like a flood of water pouring into
a deep gorge.
This is a matter of positioning.

❖ ❖ ❖

ADVANTAGE:

The concept
advantage 利
means also an
opening, *an*
opportunity, *and*
having an **edge**
in a given situ-
ation.

You can't do everything so you must choose your best opportunities over your second-best options.

Over the long term, investing in second-rate opportunities adds up to failure.

 Warriors know that their success depends upon other people. You need the overwhelming support of everyone to give your progress real momentum.

Everyone must support the right positions.

♦ ♦ ♦

ELEMENTS:

This five-step process takes knowledge of the **ground** *and converts it into what we call an* **aim** *for the future.*

Related Articles from *Sun Tzu's Playbook*

In this fourth chapter, Sun Tzu explains the process for advancing positions. To learn the step-by-step techniques involved, we recommend the Sun Tzu's Art of War Playbook *articles listed below.*

1.1.2 Defending Positions: how we defend our current positions until new positions are established.

1.2 Subobjective Positions: the subjective and objective aspects of a position.

1.3.1 Competitive Comparison: competition as the comparison of positions.

1.7 Competitive Power: the sources of superiority in challenges.

1.8 Progress Cycle: the adaptive loop by which positions are advanced.

1.8.1 Creation and Destruction: the creation and destruction of competitive positions.

1.8.2 The Adaptive Loop: the continual reiteration of position analysis.

3.0.0 Identifying Opportunities: the use of opportunities to advance a position.

3.2 Opportunity Creation: how change creates opportunities.

Chapter 5

Momentum: The Element of Surprise

How do you meet every challenge so that you are confident you will succeed? You must understand that you never have complete control over your environment. The magic of strategy is that it gives you control over unpredictable situations. To get this control, you use what Sun Tzu calls "momentum."

The term "momentum" has a very specific definition in the science of strategy. In common usage, especially sports, momentum is generally defined by the idea that past success leads to future success. While Sun Tzu would agree that momentum leads to success, he would not agree that success leads to momentum. Instead, true momentum comes from using the element of surprise.

Strategically, surprise is based upon setting expectations. If people don't know what to expect, everything is random so nothing is a surprise. You must have a standard, called direct action, that sets up the surprise or innovation based on creativity.

Innovation requires that you put together common, familiar ideas in new and interesting ways. Dependability is good, but you don't want opponents to know exactly how you will respond. It is the unpredictable that gives you power.

Every strategic encounter will take unexpected turns. The key is to prepare your surprises in advance. A warrior learns how to prepare for changes in direction and to harness them to create momentum. If you are prepared for the unexpected and your opponents are not, you can take control of a confused situation.

Momentum

SUN TZU SAID:

You control a large group the same as you control a few. 1
You just divide their ranks correctly.
You fight a large army the same as you fight a small one.
You only need the right position and communication.
You may meet a large enemy army.
You must be able to sustain an enemy attack without being
defeated.
You must correctly use both surprise and direct
action.
Your army's position must increase your strength.
Troops flanking an enemy can smash them like
eggs.
You must correctly use both strength and
weakness.

STRAIGHT

The character
straight 正 also
means correct,
normal, and
even. Its oppo-
site is unusual,
奇, strange, and
odd.

It is the same in all battles. 2
You use a direct approach to engage the
enemy.
You use surprise to win.

The Element of Surprise

THE WARRIOR HEARS:

1 Warriors are not intimidated by the size of a challenge.
The secret is breaking tasks down into manageable steps.
You solve large problems by addressing a series of smaller ones.
You advance your position gradually while gathering information.
An unexpected tragedy can blindside you.
If you do not panic, you can survive any setback without being crushed by it.
You must create expectations but then go beyond what is expected.
You must use the resources of your existing position.
You can find surprisingly easy ways around even difficult problems.
Within every problem, you must look for a hidden opportunity.

SURPRISE:

*Because no con-
frontation goes
as planned, and
can always go
badly, you must
prepare surpris-
es beforehand.*

2 Warriors have a system for meeting challenges.
They always face their problems directly.
They solve their problems creatively.

4You must use surprise for a successful invasion.
Surprise is as infinite as the weather and land.
Surprise is as inexhaustible as the flow of a river.

7You can be stopped and yet recover the initiative.
You must use your days and months correctly.

FIVE:

Five 五key *elements of two pairs balanced around a center describe every area in Chinese science, including strategy.*

9If you are defeated, you can recover.
You must use the four seasons correctly.

11There are only a few notes in the scale.
Yet you can always rearrange them.
You can never hear every song of victory.

14There are only a few basic colors.
Yet you can always mix them.
You can never see all the shades of victory.

17There are only a few flavors.
Yet you can always blend them.
You can never taste all the flavors of victory.

20You fight with momentum.
There are only a few types of surprises and direct actions.
Yet you can always vary the ones you use.
There is no limit to the ways you can win.

24Surprise and direct action give birth to each other.
They are like a circle without end.
You cannot exhaust all their possible combinations!

You improve your position by being creative.
Use your environment and its changes to fuel your ideas.
You will never run out of creative new innovations.

When you have a setback, you can regain your momentum.
You must invest your time in your best options.

You can make progress even after a disaster.
It takes time to get back what you have lost.

Old ideas may sound tired and familiar.
You spark new ideas by playing with old ones.
Everything you hear can be a source of inspiration.

No situation is ever as simple as black and white.
The key to creativity is finding a new point of view.
The world never runs out of new valuable visions.

VARIETY:

Even though everything consists of only five key elements, those elements can be arranged in an endless number of chains.

You have a limited number of ingredients with which to work.
However, there is no limit to how you can put them together.
This is why your human potential is infinite.

Momentum comes from exceeding expectations.
Neither surprising people nor setting expectations is complicated.
People expect you to react as you have before.
By escaping from your habits, you give yourself momentum.

Expectations enable surprise, and surprise changes expectations.
Each element makes the other possible.
Continually shaping expectations makes new surprises possible.

Surging water flows together rapidly. 3
Its pressure washes away boulders.
This is momentum.

4A hawk suddenly strikes a bird.
Its contact alone kills the prey.
This is timing.

7You must fight only winning battles.
Your momentum must be overwhelming.
Your timing must be exact.

10Your momentum is like the tension of a bent crossbow.
Your timing is like the pulling of a trigger.

War is very complicated and confusing. 4
Battle is chaotic.
Nevertheless, you must not allow chaos.

4War is very sloppy and messy.
Positions turn around.
Nevertheless, you must never be defeated.

7Chaos gives birth to control.
Fear gives birth to courage.
Weakness gives birth to strength.

3 The pressure of change comes from its speed.
Continuous change wears away any obstacle.
Momentum depends on change.

The force of surprise comes from its suddenness.
Its revelation alone creates a moment of truth.
Pick the right moment to use it.

You cannot afford to take any challenge lightly.
Momentum must be clearly on your side.
Know exactly when a sudden change is required.

You use the pace of change to pressure opponents.
A sudden surprise collapses that pressure all at once.

4 Your choices are seldom obvious.
Unexpected issues arise.
Your job is to see patterns in the messiness.

Real-life situations are not clean and predictable.
Events change your position.
Still,

Only unpredictable change creates major opportunities.
Facing the unknown requires us to make choices.
Warriors recognize their limitations, which enables them to succeed.

¹⁰You must control chaos.
This depends on your planning.
Your men must brave their fears.
This depends on their momentum.

¹⁴You have strengths and weaknesses.
These come from your position.

¹⁶You must force the enemy to move to your advantage.
Use your position.
The enemy must follow you.
Surrender a position.
The enemy must take it.
You can offer an advantage to move him.
You can use your men to move him.
You can use your strength to hold him.

REVERSAL:

In the natural process, each element cre- ates or gives **birth** 生 *to its complementary opposite if given enough time.*

You want a successful battle. 5
To do this, you must seek momentum.
Do not just demand a good fight from your people.
You must pick good people and then give them momentum.

You must prepare for confusion.

You must leave room in your plans for the unexpected.

Warriors are not threatened by a surprising development.

They use surprise to increase their momentum.

You must know what you can do and what you cannot do.

As you advance your position, your capabilities will change.

You use challenges to move others to set up an opportunity.

Act as they expect you to act.

They will react based on their assumptions.

Give others something they value.

They must take what they are given.

You offer an advantage to create your own advantage.

Your efforts can win others to your side.

Keep them on your side by focusing your efforts.

5 You want to meet challenges successfully.
You must have the feeling you are winning.
Winning is never a matter of just working harder or longer.
You must know the right methods and use them creatively.

CHAOS:

War defines a competitive environment in which combatants' plans collide resulting in something that no one plans.

⁵You must create momentum.
You create it with your men during battle.
This is comparable to rolling trees and stones.
Trees and stones roll because of their shape and weight.
Offer men safety and they will stay calm.
Endanger them and they will act.
Give them a place and they will hold.
Round them up and they will march.

¹³You make your men powerful in battle with momentum.
This should be like rolling round stones down over a high,
steep cliff.
Momentum is critical.

INFLUENCE:

The concept of **influence 勢** *or* **momentum** *combines characters meaning* **force** *or* **power力** *, with the character for* **ground 地***.*

You must create a sense of moving forward.

You create it when you are compared to others.

People act predictably based on their personality and position.

People act according to their personality and their self-interest.

If nothing changes, people will do what they have always done.

People will act only if they are afraid of losing something.

People will stand if they have something to defend.

When people are in a group, they follow the example of others.

Warriors know how to succeed by using the element of surprise.

You work to set up a surprise by getting everything in the right position beforehand.

Momentum shifts the situation in your favor.

MOMENTUM:

By definition, momentum does not come from doing what is predicted, but from doing something that no one expects.

Related Articles from *Sun Tzu's Playbook*

In his fifth chapter, Sun Tzu explains the process for creating momentum. To learn the step-by-step techniques involved, we recommend the Sun Tzu's Art of War Playbook *articles listed below.*

1.2 Subobjective Positions: the subjective and objective aspects of a position.

7.0 Creating Momentum: how momentum requires creativity.

7.1 Order from Chaos: the value of chaos in creating competitive momentum.

7.1.1 Creating Surprise: creating surprise using our chaotic environment.

7.1.2 Momentum Psychology: the psychology of surprise.

7.1.3 Standards and Innovation: the methodology of creativity.

7.2 Standards First: the role of standards in creating connections with others.

7.2.1 Proven Methods: identifying and recognizing the limits of best practices.

7.2.2 Preparing Expectations: how we shape other people's expectations.

7.3 Strategic Innovation: a simple system for innovation.

7.3.1 Expected Elements: dividing processes and systems into components.

7.3.2 Elemental Rearrangement: seeing invention as rearranging proven elements.

7.3.3 Creative Innovation: the more advanced methods for innovation.

7.4 Competitive Timing: the role of timing in creating momentum.

7.4.1 Timing Methods: the three simplest methods of controlling timing.

7.4.2 Momentum Timing: the relative value of momentum at various times in a campaign.

7.4.3 Interrupting Patterns: how repetition creates patterns for surprise.

7.5 Momentum Limitations: the implications of momentum's temporary nature.

7.5.1 Momentum Conversion: converting momentum into positions with more value.

7.5.2 The Spread of Innovation: the spread of innovation to advance our position.

7.6 Productive Competition: using momentum to produce more resources.

7.6.1 Resource Discovery: using innovation to create value from seemingly worthless resources.

7.6.2 Ground Creation: the creation of new competitive ground to be successful.

Chapter 6

Weakness and Strength: The Alchemy of Opposites

Strategy requires constantly improving your position. To continually make progress in a competitive world, you must leverage your strengths against your rivals' weaknesses. Sun Tzu teaches the secret for accomplishing this using the alchemy of opposites. The rule of opposites teaches that if you seek out emptiness, you will find fullness, and if you seek out weakness, you will find strength.

The first application of this rule is choosing a battleground. Regular people follow the crowd, so warriors do the opposite. They seek new, unexplored areas.

Emptiness creates speed. Warriors go around obstacles instead of wasting time struggling with them. You want to maintain your opponents' ignorance about your plans, so warriors avoid talking about their goals. Braggarts make themselves easy targets because they are so full of themselves.

Focus or concentration is a form of fullness, while division is a form of emptiness. Everything that is put together from separate parts has seams of emptiness or weakness. You concentrate your efforts at those weak points to generate strength.

Since opposites tend to replace each other, situations are fluid. What was once empty becomes full and what was full is emptied. Warriors change their positions as these shifts warrant. Success goes to those who can adjust to these changes most quickly. Every window of opportunity that opens is open for only a limited time. You must act instantly before others know what you are doing.

Weakness and Strength

SUN TZU SAID:

Always arrive first to the empty battlefield to await the 1
enemy at your leisure.
After the battleground is occupied and you hurry to it,
fighting is more difficult.

3You want a successful battle.
Move your men, but not into opposing forces.

5You can make enemies come to you.
Offer them an advantage.
You can make enemies avoid coming to you.
Threaten them with danger.

EMPTY & FULL

The concepts
empty 處 *(poor,*
scarce) and **full**
壹 *(rich, abun-*
dant*)* are condi-
tions affecting
every element of
a position.

9When enemies are fresh, you can tire them.
When they are well fed, you can starve them.
When they are relaxed, you can move them.

The Alchemy of Opposites

THE WARRIOR HEARS:

1 Warriors are pioneers who discover new areas and keep ahead
of the crowd.
Regular people follow the crowd and put themselves in constant
competition with others.

You want to make progress easily.
Move forward where other people leave openings.

You sometimes want your rivals to follow your lead.
You must leave an opening for them.
You can also keep your opponents from copying you.
You must deny them any opening.

CHANGE:

For everyone, fullness is only a temporary state.
As much as people have, they will soon want more.
Even the most comfortable people can be moved.

*The key ele-
ment of cli-
mate (heaven)
dictates that
positions natu-
rally progress
from strength to
weakness.*

Leave any place without haste. 2
Hurry to where you are unexpected.
You can easily march hundreds of miles without tiring.
To do so, travel through areas that are deserted.
You must take whatever you attack.
Attack when there is no defense.
You must have walls to defend.
Defend where it is impossible to attack.

⁹Be skilled in attacking.
Give the enemy no idea where to defend.

¹¹Be skillful in your defense.
Give the enemy no idea where to attack.

Be subtle! Be subtle! 3
Arrive without any clear formation.
Ghostly! Ghostly!
Arrive without a sound.
You must use all your skill to control enemies'
decisions.

⁶Advance where they can't defend.
Charge through their openings.
Withdraw where enemies cannot chase you.
Move quickly so that they cannot catch you.

MOVEMENT:

*In moving, emptiness is **advance** 攻, moving into another's territory, and fullness is **defense** 守, holding your existing territory.*

2 Warriors are slow to give up what they have.
However, you must utilize unexpected openings instantly.
If you are going in the right direction, you feel energized.
The right direction always leads away from the crowd.
When you move into new areas, commit yourself to success.
Avoid obstacles that will slow you down.
Establish a strong position when you stake out a claim.
This discourages others from challenging you.

Continually search out new opportunities.
Keep everyone guessing about what you will do next.

Take nothing you have for granted.
Discover your weaknesses before your opponents do.

3 Warriors keep their opponents ignorant.
You must never signal what you intend to accomplish.
Maintain the mystery.
Move into new areas quietly.
Success comes from controlling the perceptions
of others.

Move forward where no one is threatened..
Windows of opportunity do not remain open.
Move into areas where others cannot go.
You must keep ahead of the crowd.

STEALTH:

All methods
connect to the
key pieces of
knowledge: that
is, the time and
place of battle.
Information
controls the
battle.

[10]Always pick your own battles.
Enemies can hide behind high walls and deep trenches.
Do not try to win by fighting them directly.
Instead, attack a place that they must recapture.
Avoid the battles that you don't want.
You can divide the ground and yet defend it.
Don't give enemies anything to win.
Divert them by coming to where you defend.

Make other men take a position while you take none. 4
Then focus your forces where enemies divide their forces.
Where you focus, you unite your forces.
When enemies divide, they create many small groups.
You want your large group to attack one of their small ones.
Then you have many men where enemies have but a few.
Your larger force can overwhelm a small one.
Then go on to the next small enemy group.
You can take them one at a time.

You must keep the place that you have 5
chosen as a battleground a secret.
Enemies must not know it.
Force enemies to prepare their defense in
many places.
You want enemies to defend many places.
Then you can choose where to fight.
Their forces will be weak there.

METHODS:

*In methods,
emptiness is the
division 分 *of*
few 寡 *forces,
and fullness is
the* **concentra-
tion** 專 *of a*
crowd 眾 *of
forces.*

You always have good options.

Some desirable positions are extremely well protected.

Going after these positions is a recipe for failure.

Instead, go after desirable positions that others have ignored.

No one can force you into a fight.

Define your territory in a way that makes it easy to protect.

No one should benefit from attacking you.

Make it clear that there is nothing for them to win.

4 Warriors are flexible while others take rigid positions.

Warriors find the holes in the positions taken by others.

You must concentrate your efforts on one opportunity at a time.

Regular people get scattered among too many areas.

Your concentration on one area makes your rivals easy to beat.

Warriors apply all their resources toward the immediate challenge.

Concentrated efforts succeed where diluted efforts fail.

Tackle small, distracted opponents one after another.

Each small success adds up to progress.

5 Warriors do not talk about where they plan to focus their efforts next.

Keep your priorities to yourself.

Regular people are unable to decide upon their priorities.

They defend everything they do as important.

Choose challenges that other people avoid.

You will encounter little opposition.

PLACES:

Place *and* **ground** *are defined elsewhere in Sun Tzu as infinite. By this logic, there are always places that are empty and unguarded.*

7If they reinforce their front lines, they deplete their rear.
If they reinforce their rear, they deplete their front.
If they reinforce their right flank, they deplete their left.
If they reinforce their left flank, they deplete their right.
Without knowing the place of attack, they cannot prepare.
Without knowing the right place, they will be weak everywhere.

13Your enemies have weak points.
Prepare your men against them.
Your enemies have strong points.
Make their men prepare themselves against you.

You must know the battleground. 6
You must know the time of battle.
You can then travel a thousand miles and still win the battle.

4The enemy should not know the battleground.
He shouldn't know the time of battle.
His left flank will be unable to support his right.
His right will be unable to support his left.
His front lines will be unable to support his rear.
His rear will be unable to support his front.
His support is distant even if it is only ten miles away.
What unknown place can be close?

GROUND:

In the measurement of the ground, emptiness or weakness is what is distant 遠, while fullness or strength is what is near 近.

Regular people are always shifting their priorities.
They are easily distracted by every passing fashion.
They jump from one thing to another.
The result is that they are always out of balance.
Regular people never identify what they must focus on.
They never accomplish anything.

Everyone has gaps in his or her abilities.
Target the gaps your opponents leave you.
Everyone excels at some things.
They cannot defend their strengths if you don't attack them.

6 Warriors pick challenges on ground they know.
You must select a time that is in your favor.
You can go any distance when success there is certain.

Focus on situations in which others are poorly informed.
Pick meetings in which others are unprepared.
If people are ill informed, they cannot act quickly.
If people cannot act, they will remain ignorant. .
When things fail to go as planned, people don't know what to do next.
Not knowing what to do, no one can make plans. .
Ignorance creates obstacles to every reasonable response.
Ignorance makes every task difficult.

DIRECTIONS:

In another analogy, the four directions here, left, right, front, and back, are connected to the four key externals elements of a position.

12You control the balance of forces.
The enemy may have many men but they are superfluous.
How can they help him to victory?

15We say:
You must let victory happen.

17The enemy may have many men.
You can still control him without a fight.

When you form your strategy, know the strengths and 7
weaknesses of your plan.
When you execute a plan, know how to manage both action
and inaction.
When you take a position, know the deadly and the winning
grounds.
When you enter into battle, know when you have too many
or too few men.

5Use your position as your war's centerpiece.
Arrive at the battle without a formation.
Don't take a position in advance.
Then even the best spies can't report it.
Even the wisest general cannot plan to counter you.
Take a position where you can triumph using superior numbers.
Keep opposing forces ignorant.
Everyone should learn your location after your position has
given you success.
No one should know how your location gives you a winning
position.

You alone know when and where you must act.
Pick a battle when your opponents' resources are unavailable.
Your knowledge is the key to your success.

Pay attention.
Pick your opportunities wisely.

It doesn't matter how powerful your opponents are.
They can't fight what they don't understand.

7 Warriors factor in the advantages and disadvantages of their position in planning every move.
No plan is perfect, but you must know when action is better than doing nothing.
No position is perfect, but you must know which directions lead to success and which to failure.
You must choose the challenges that are best suited to your capabilities.

Your strategic position is your central asset.
When meeting a new challenge, wait before committing yourself.
Don't give away your intentions.
Keep your opponents in the dark as long as possible.
Do not give people time to prepare to act against you.
Focus all your efforts on one thing at one time to achieve success.
Don't let others know what to expect.
Others should know where you are headed only after it is too late to stop you.
Others should understand your opportunity only after it is too late to undermine it.

Make a successful battle one from which the enemy cannot
recover.
You must continually adjust your position to his position.

Manage your military position like water. **8**
Water takes every shape.
It avoids the high and moves to the low.
Your war can take any shape.
It must avoid the strong and strike the weak.
Water follows the shape of the land that directs its flow.
Your forces follow the enemy, who determines how you win.

LEADERSHIP:

LEADERSHIP:

*In making a
decision, you
use empty/full
the same that
water does: it
flows naturally
from fullness
to emptiness,
or from what is
high* 高*, down to
the* low 下*.*

[8]Make war without a standard approach.
Water has no consistent shape.
If you follow the enemy's shifts and changes,
you can always find a way to win.
We call this shadowing.

[12]Fight five different campaigns without a
firm rule for victory.
Use all four seasons without a consistent
position.
Your timing must be sudden.
A few weeks determine your failure or
success.

♦ ♦ ♦

People can hamper your progress only if you give them the opportunity to do so.

You must be faster and more flexible than your opponents.

8 Warriors are infinitely adaptable.
You can adjust to every situation.
Find success by following the path of least resistance.
Success can take an infinite number of forms.
You must avoid obstacles and move into openings.
You must understand your position and leverage it.
You embrace problems because they are the source of opportunity.

Your progress will take different forms.
Consistent progress requires constant change.
If you look for new challenges, you will inevitably discover opportunities to advance.
Keep close to good information sources.

Invest in advancing in all five aspects of your position in different ways.,
As you move forward, new possibilities emerge with time.
Act instantly when opportunities arise.
In a short time, you can change your entire situation.

AWARDS:

Our many books adapting Sun Tzu's lessons have won awards in business, careers, self-help, sports, philosophy, and youth nonfiction.

Related Articles from *Sun Tzu's Playbook*

In chapter six, Sun Tzu explains how to find opportunities by leveraging opposites. To learn the step-by-step techniques involved, we recommend the Sun Tzu's Art of War Playbook *articles listed below.*

1.2.1 Competitive Landscapes: the arenas in which rivals jockey for position.

1.2.2 Exploiting Exploration: how competitive landscapes are searched and positions utilized.

1.2.3 Position Complexity: how strategic positions arise from interactions in complex environments.

1.3.1 Competitive Comparison: competition as the comparison of positions.

2.4 Contact Networks: the range of contacts needed to create perspective.

2.4.1 Ground Perspective: getting information on a new competitive arena.

2.4.2 Climate Perspective: getting perspective on temporary external conditions.

2.4.3 Command Perspective: developing sources for understanding decision-makers.

2.4.4 Methods Perspective: developing contacts who understand best practices.

2.4.5 Mission Perspective: how we develop and use a perspective on motivation.

2.5 The Big Picture: building big-picture strategic awareness.

2.6 Knowledge Leverage: getting competitive value out of knowledge.

2.7 Information Secrecy: the role of limiting information in controlling relationships.

3.2.3 Complementary Opposites: the dynamics of balance from opposing forces.

Chapter 7

Armed Conflict: The Suppression of Hostility

Good strategy dictates that you avoid unnecessary confrontations because it makes success too costly. The more conflict you have in life, the less likely your success becomes. However, when confrontations are unavoidable, good strategy positions you to deal with them successfully.

Sun Tzu begins this chapter by explaining that confrontations are best avoided. Your real opportunities lie in taking your own path, distancing yourself from the crowd. This approach naturally avoids most forms of direct confrontation. The focus of strategy is continual progress, not beating others. Speed is important to progress, and confrontations with others only slow you down.

You cannot force a favorable showdown with rivals or opponents. When you obviously want a showdown, your opponents are going to do their best to avoid you. Instead, you must lull opponents into a false sense of security. You confuse the situation so that rivals are unprepared for your opposition.

Communication is often the key to winning unavoidable confrontations. Who wins or loses a confrontation largely depends other people taking sides. The role of good communication is to get as many people on your side as possible.

Warriors choose the right time and place for unavoidable confrontations. You must be patient enough to wait until everything is in your favor. You must also remember that your goal is to remove an opponent as an obstacle, not to make him or her fight you.

Armed Conflict

Everyone uses the arts of war. 1
You accept orders from the government.
Then you assemble your army.
You organize your men and build camps.
You must avoid disasters from armed conflict.

⁶Seeking armed conflict can be disastrous.
Because of this, a detour can be the shortest
path.
Because of this, problems can become opportunities.

⁹Use an indirect route as your highway.
Use the search for advantage to guide you.
When you fall behind, you must catch up.
When you get ahead, you must wait.
You must know the detour that most directly
accomplishes your plan.

CONFLICT

Conflict 争 *is defined as the intentional use of violence, which isn't necessarily required to be successful* **battle** 戰 *or* **war** 軍.

The Suppression of Hostility

THE WARRIOR HEARS:

1 Everyone tries to think strategically.
Everyone has to meet obligations to other people.
Everyone puts together resources.
Everyone organizes his or her efforts and chooses positions.
Warriors alone know how to avoid senseless confrontations.

Only fools see confrontations to prove themselves.
Going out of your way to avoid confrontation is the
path to success.
Avoiding confrontations uncovers new ways to make
progress.

You should never go after what you want directly.
You must look for opportunities, not showdowns.
Setbacks are temporary.
Don't get ahead of yourself.
You can learn the best way around opponents that
stand in your path.

AVOIDANCE:

In Sun Tzu's sys-
tem, all conflict
is costly, so you
seek to avoid
conflict and
develop posi-
tions that win
without it.

[14]Undertake armed conflict when you have an advantage. Seeking armed conflict for its own sake is dangerous.

You can build up an army to fight for an advantage. 2
Then you won't catch the enemy.
You can force your army to go fight for an advantage.
Then you abandon your heavy supply wagons.

[5]You keep only your armor and hurry after the enemy.
You avoid stopping day or night.
You use many roads at the same time.
You go hundreds of miles to fight for an advantage.
Then the enemy catches your commanders and your army.
Your strong soldiers get there first.
Your weaker soldiers follow behind.
Using this approach, only one in ten will arrive.
You can try to go fifty miles to fight for an advantage.
Then your commanders and army will stumble.
Using this method, only half of your soldiers will make it.
You can try to go thirty miles to fight for an advantage.
Then only two out of three will get there.

[18]If you make your army travel without good supply lines, your army will die.
Without supplies and food, your army will die.
If you don't save the harvest, your army will die.

ADVANTAGE:

The two-character sequence **conflict** 爭 **advantage** 利 *means using violence in the attempt to create superiority over an enemy.*

Only confront people directly when you must do so to win.
Challenging people for fun is destructive.

2 Warriors do not attempt to pursue a decisive showdown.
Your opponents can easily avoid these situations.
It is always a mistake to chase after any confrontation.
Your impatience undermines your support from others.

No armor can defend you from your own impatience.
Speed is dangerous when it wearies you.
Speed is dangerous when it divides you.
Impatience for a showdown tempts you to overextend yourself.
When you are overextended, you are likely to make bad choices.
You may start off strong.
However, you will finish poorly.
Nine times out of ten, overextending yourself leads to failure.
Impatience for a showdown puts you off balance.
Then you are more inclined to make mistakes.
Being off balance always depletes your resources.
Impatience for a showdown takes you out of position.
Being out of position always weakens you.

Warriors don't look for fights when fighting will undermine their long-term support from others.
Warriors don't look for fights that strain their resources.
Warriors don't look for fights that cannot enrich them.

SUPPLIES:

War is less about fighting than understanding how conditions change over time. Without supplies, your ability to fight disappears.

21Do not let any of your potential enemies know what you are planning.

Still, you must not hesitate to form alliances.
You must know the mountains and forests.
You must know where the obstructions are.
You must know where the marshes are.
If you don't, you cannot move the army.
If you don't, you must use local guides.
If you don't, you can't take advantage of the terrain.

You make war by making a false stand. 3
By finding an advantage, you can move.
By dividing and joining, you can reinvent yourself and transform the situation.
You can move as quickly as the wind.
You can rise like the forest.
You can invade and plunder like fire.
You can stay as motionless as a mountain.
You can be as mysterious as the fog.
You can strike like sounding thunder.

NOBLEMEN:

Sun Tzu uses the term **various** 諸 **noblemen** 侯 *to indicate other people in a situation who are potentially either allies or enemies.*

10Divide your troops to plunder the villages.
When on open ground, dividing is an advantage.

Don't worry about organization; just move.
Be the first to find a new route that leads directly to a winning plan.
This is how you are successful at armed conflict.

You must not let potential opponents think that you want to fight with them.

Instead, your first goal is to make them your friends.

By getting close to them, you learn their strengths and secrets.

You need to know where they might hamper your progress.

You need to learn where you might get stuck.

Without this knowledge, progress is impossible.

To get this information, you need to be close to your enemies.

Use your knowledge to strengthen your position.

3 A warrior's success depends on manipulating appearances.

You must have the patience to uncover the right opportunities.

You can catch your opponents off balance if you can change the way a situation looks.

Use speed to confuse your opponents.

Use surprise to confuse your opponents.

Confusion allows you to move forward and accumulate resources.

Confusion allows you to stand and defend your position.

The secret is keeping your opponents in the dark.

Surprise leads to quick successes.

You can divide your efforts to make money.

You are looking for opportunities, try many things is helpful.

Don't worry about planning, just get out there.

Speed is the secrets to finding out what you can do to be successful.

This is how you win when facing direct challenges from others.

REPETITION:

While the English translation makes sections of the text seem repetitive, there are important changes in meaning from the context.

Military experience says: 4
"You can speak, but you will not be heard.
You must use gongs and drums.
You cannot really see your forces just by looking.
You must use banners and flags."

6You must master gongs, drums, banners, and flags.
Place people as a single unit where they can all see and hear.
You must unite them as one.
Then the brave cannot advance alone.
The fearful cannot withdraw alone.
You must force them to act as a group.

12In night battles, you must use numerous fires and drums.
In day battles, you must use many banners and flags.
You must position your people to control what they see and
hear.

You control your army by controlling its morale. 5
As a general, you must be able to control emotions.

3In the morning, a person's energy is high.
During the day, it fades.
By evening, a person's thoughts turn to home.
You must use your troops wisely.
Avoid the enemy's high spirits.
Strike when his men are lazy and want to go home.
This is how you master energy.

4 Warriors learn from experience.
You should never expect people to listen to you.
You must work hard to get attention.
You cannot let yourself be confused by complex appearances.
You need a framework for organizing your efforts.

Communication is the key to controlling confrontations.
You must control what others see and hear.
You need other people on your side.
If you are too aggressive, you alienate some people.
If you are too timid, you lose the support of others.
You must offer people a mission that brings them together.

You need the right communication to suit your situation.
You change your methods as the situation changes.
You must expect others to interpret their situation based upon their position.

5 Warriors maintain a positive attitude.
You can only win confrontations by controlling your emotions.

Conserve your energy before a confrontation.
You must avoid tiring yourself.
Gear up for a confrontation when your opponent wants it least.
Husband your energy.
Opponents fight more adamantly early in the day.
If you wait until later in the day, they will want to back down.
Match your vigor against an opponent's weariness.

¹⁰Use discipline to await the chaos of battle.
Keep relaxed to await a crisis.
This is how you master emotion.

¹³Stay close to home to await the distant enemy.
Stay comfortable to await the weary enemy.
Stay well fed to await the hungry enemy.
This is how you master power.

Don't entice the enemy when his ranks are orderly. 6
You must not attack when his formations are solid.
This is how you master adaptation.

BY MEANS OF:

The character translated as **by means of** 以 *indicates the prescription for a given situation. For most situations, the rule uses empty/ full opposites.*

⁴You must follow these military rules.
Do not take a position facing the high ground.
Do not oppose those with their backs to the wall.
Do not follow those who pretend to flee.
Do not attack the enemy's strongest men.
Do not swallow the enemy's bait.
Do not block an army that is heading home.
Leave an escape outlet for a surrounded army.
Do not press a desperate foe.
This is how you use military skills.

✦ ✦ ✦

Confrontations take unpredictable turns.
Stay calm when things appear to go wrong.
Match your composure against your opponent's agitation.

Plan confrontations in a place that favors you.
Plan confrontations at a time that favors you.
Plan confrontations when your opponents are out of gas.
This is how you assure a successful showdown.

6 Warriors avoid the mistake of overconfidence.
You must avoid confrontations with well-prepared opponents.
Your success depends only upon your flexibility.

Master the moves in the play book of competition.
Never fight against people who are in a superior position.
When people are desperate, they are at their most dangerous.
Avoid the temptation to overextend yourself.
Aim only at your challenger's weaknesses.
See through the deceptions of others.
Allow other people the leave you the openings you need.
Give people an easy way to save face in a conflict.
Pressuring the desperate creates explosions.
This is the skill of managing confrontations.

INACTION:

The best possible response to a situation can be inaction, because it costs nothing. Sun Tzu warns against what might be called the prejudice toward action.

Related Articles from *Sun Tzu's Playbook*

In chapter seven, Sun Tzu teaches us to focus on building positions instead of on tearing down opponents. To learn the step-by-step techniques involved, we recommend the Sun Tzu's Art of War Playbook *articles listed below.*

1.2.1 Competitive Landscapes: the arenas in which rivals jockey for position.

1.3.1 Competitive Comparison: competition as the comparison of positions.

1.5 Competing Agents: characteristics of competitors.

1.7 Competitive Power: the sources of superiority in challenges.

1.8.1 Creation and Destruction: the creation and destruction of competitive positions.

1.9 Competition and Production: the two opposing skill sets of competition and production.

2.1.3 Strategic Deception: misinformation and disinformation in competition.

2.6 Knowledge Leverage: getting competitive value out of knowledge.

2.7 Information Secrecy: the role of secrecy in relationships.

3.1 Strategic Economics: balancing the cost and benefits of positioning.

3.1.1 Resource Limitations: the inherent limitation of strategic resources.

3.1.3 Conflict Cost: the costly nature of resolving competitive comparisons by conflict.

3.1.6 Time Limitations: understanding the time limits on opportunities.

3.7 Defining the Ground: redefining a competitive arena to create relative mismatches.

4.7 Competitive Weakness: how certain opportunities can bring out our weaknesses.

6.1.2 Prioritizing Conditions: parsing complex competitive conditions into simple responses.

6.8 Competitive Psychology: improving competitive psychology even in adversity and failure.

7.4 Competitive Timing: the role of timing in creating momentum.

7.6 Productive Competition: using momentum to produce more resources.

7.6.2 Ground Creation: the creation of new competitive ground to be successful.

8.5 Leveraging Emotions: how we use emotion to obtain rewards.

9.5.2 Avoiding Emotion: the danger of exploiting environmental vulnerabilities for purely emotion reasons.

Chapter 8

Adaptability: The Mastery of Change

Strategy is a process of continually adjusting to change. Warriors are sensitive to changes in their environment and continually adjust to them. Regular people pay very little attention to what is happening around them and tend to react in the same ways regardless of their situation. In Sun Tzu's view, successful strategy must be dynamic and be based on the willingness to change.

Warriors are masters of change. This chapter serves as an introduction to the next three chapters, which describe a number of specific situations, how to recognize them, and how to respond to them. Regular people have two problems in responding appropriately to the changing situation. Either they fail to recognize opportunities or they fail to take advantage of those opportunities.

Warriors make a habit of change while regular people are unable to change their habits. Though it seems counterintuitive, you must change to be consistent because consistency requires continually adapting to a changing world.

In dealing with change, the best defense is a good offense. If you don't leverage the opportunities of a changing world, others will almost certainly use those changes against you.

The biggest risk in adjusting to change comes from the flaws in your character. Your best qualities can become dangerous when they are taken to extremes. An increased pace of change pressures you toward those extremes.

Adaptability

SUN TZU SAID:

Everyone uses the arts of war. 1
As a general, you get your orders from the government.
You gather your troops.
On dangerous ground, you must not camp.
Where the roads intersect, you must join your allies.
When an area is cut off, you must not delay in it.
When you are surrounded, you must scheme.
In a life-or-death situation, you must fight.
There are roads that you must not take.
There are armies that you must not fight.
There are strongholds that you must not attack.
There are positions that you must not defend.
There are government commands that must
not be obeyed.

NINE:

The number **nine** *丿乚 is sometimes used to mean* **many**, *but it also combines the key five elements with the four steps in Sun Tzu's system.*

[14]Military leaders must be experts in knowing
how to adapt to find an advantage.
This will teach you the use of war.

The Mastery of Change

THE WARRIOR HEARS:

1 Warriors are responsive to their situation.
You always have someone in authority over you.
You always need to assemble resources.
In risky situations, you cannot pretend you are safe.
When the risks are shared, you cannot act like you are alone.
When a path leads nowhere, you must get off it.
When you face overwhelming odds, you can still find an opening.
Fighting is necessary only when you run out of options.
You must know where your decisions lead.
Avoid making the wrong enemies.
Avoid the most difficult battles.
Change your mind rather than defend bad decisions.
Know when doing what you have been told will be a mistake.

ADAPTING:

Warriors train themselves to recognize their situation so they know the best way to react.
Your good judgment is necessary in competition.

This chapter and its list of ten situations refer to the following three chapters, which give many conditions and their responses.

[16]Some commanders are not good at making adjustments to find an advantage.
They can know the shape of the terrain.
Still, they cannot find an advantageous position.

[19]Some military commanders do not know how to adjust their methods.
They can find an advantageous position.
Still, they cannot use their men effectively.

You must be creative in your planning. 2
You must adapt to your opportunities and weaknesses.
You can use a variety of approaches and still have a consistent result.
You must adjust to a variety of problems and consistently solve them.

You can deter your potential enemy by using his 3 weaknesses against him.
You can keep your potential enemy's army busy by giving it work to do.
You can rush your potential enemy by offering him an advantageous position.

VARIETY:

In competitive situations, **variety 雜** *keeps opponents guessing. In controlled environments,* **reliability 恃** *maintains consistency.*

You must make use of war. 4
Do not trust that the enemy isn't coming.
Trust your readiness to meet him.
Do not trust that the enemy won't attack.
Rely only on your ability to pick a place that the enemy can't attack.

You must make some changes to highlight where your real opportunities are.

You can be very well informed.

Opportunities are hard to find in a static environment.

You cannot keep doing what you have always done and make real progress.

Seeing an opportunity is not enough.

You must change your behavior to take advantage of it.

2 Warriors are not rigid in their planning.

Do more of what works well and less of what isn't working as well.

Consistency comes from constantly improving your position, not from repeating past behavior.

The world changes every day, creating new situations that you cannot ignore.

3 Warriors know how to take the initiative to prevent others from stopping them.

You can leverage a changing situation to more easily create problems for those who oppose you.

You can prevent people from becoming opponents if you can show them other opportunities.

4 Warriors constantly prepare for challenges.

You cannot escape from opposition.

You can only position yourself to overcome it.

You cannot escape from criticism.

You can only protect yourself by taking positions that are easy to defend.

ADAPTABILITY:

Nine changes *means the ability to move in any direction, to adapt, but your actions must always address your exact situation.*

You can exploit five different faults in a leader. 5
If he is willing to die, you can kill him.
If he wants to survive, you can capture him.
He may have a quick temper.
You can then provoke him with insults.
If he has a delicate sense of honor, you can disgrace him.
If he loves his people, you can create problems for him.
In every situation, look for these five weaknesses.
They are common faults in commanders.
They always lead to military disaster.

11To overturn an army, you must kill its general.
To do this, you must use these five weaknesses.
You must always look for them.

✦ ✦ ✦

BORN:

The character **born** 生 *as a verb means* **to begin, to start, to give birth to,** *and* **to create.** *Sun Tzu uses it to describe how one condition gives rise to a following condition.*

5 Warriors know that strengths can turn into weaknesses.
Courage is good, but too much courage is foolhardy.
Caution is good, but too much caution leads to paralysis.
Strategy demands a speedy response.
However, you cannot afford to react emotionally.
Set high standards, but perfectionists are easily frustrated.
Trusting people is good, but dependency is dangerous.
Neither you nor your opponents are perfect.
An opponent's weakness is your opportunity.
Your weakness is an opponent's opportunity.

If you fail, it is because you made poor decisions.
Flaws in your character lead to poor decisions.
Be honest about your weaknesses.

EXCESS:

*The five flaws
of a leader
relate to the five
characteristics
of a leader (see
chapter 1);
they are not the
absence of those
strengths but the
results of their
excess.*

Related Articles from *Sun Tzu's Playbook*

In chapter eight, Sun Tzu teaches us the need to constantly adapt to the situation. To learn the step-by-step techniques involved, we recommend the Sun Tzu's Art of War Playbook *articles listed below.*

1.8 Progress Cycle: the adaptive loop by which positions are advanced.

1.8.1 Creation and Destruction : the creation and destruction of competitive positions.

1.8.2 The Adaptive Loop: the continual reiteration of position analysis.

1.8.3 Cycle Time: the importance of speed in feedback and reaction.

1.8.4 Probabilistic Process: the role of chance in strategic processes and systems.

4.7.1 Command Weaknesses: the character flaws of leaders and how to exploit them.

5.2.1 Choosing Adaptability: choosing actions that allow us a maximum of future flexibility.

5.2.2 Campaign Methods: the use of campaigns and their methods.

5.2.3 Unplanned Steps: distinguishing campaign adjustments from steps in a plan.

5.3 Reaction Time: the use of speed in choosing actions.

5.3.1 Speed and Quickness: the use of pace within a dynamic environment.

6.0 Situation Response: selecting the actions most appropriate to a situation.

6.1 Situation Recognition: situation recognition in making advances.

6.1.1 Conditioned Reflexes: how we develop automatic, instantaneous responses.

6.1.2 Prioritizing Conditions: parsing complex competitive conditions into simple responses.

6.2 Campaign Evaluation: how we justify continued investment in an ongoing campaign.

6.2.1 Campaign Flow: seeing campaigns as a series of situations that flow logically from one to another.

6.2.2 Campaign Goals: assessing the value of a campaign by a larger mission.

6.3 Campaign Patterns: how knowing campaign stages gives us insight into our situation.

6.5 Nine Responses: the best responses to the nine common competitive situations.

6.7 Tailoring to Conditions: overcoming opposition using conditions in the environment.

6.7.1 Form Adjustments: adapting our responses based on the form of the ground.

6.7.2 Size Adjustments: adapting responses based on the relative size of opposing forces.

6.7.3 Strength Adjustments: how to adapt responses based on the relative strength of opposing missions.

Chapter 9

Armed March: The Path of Progress

Success breeds opposition. This chapter teaches the skills you will need to make progress in the face of opposition. Warriors know that the key to overcoming opposition is taking the right path. Taking the right path depends on correctly diagnosing the situation and choosing the best possible way to react. When you are making progress, you continually face a variety of situations.

Strategy is situation-based. Sun Tzu categorizes situations by their unevenness, changing dynamics, and uncertainty. Different conditions demand different responses. A warrior cannot simply do as he or she pleases. A warrior only does what the situation requires. As you move into new areas, you must be aware of your changing situation, because as your situation changes, you must be prepared to meet opposition.

Principles and ethics are critical to strong positioning. Competition does not take place in a social vacuum. You need people to support you. Few people are willing to support those without ethics.

The goal is progress, but progress means change. Change creates problems. Change also creates openings for others to attack you. Warriors are cautious when they are making good progress.

To outmaneuver your opponents, you need to understand what they are doing. Warriors know that actions speak louder than words. People never do anything without a purpose. Learning strategy means understanding what motivates people. You want to use that motivation to rally people to support you.

Armed March

SUN TZU SAID:

Anyone moving an army must adjust to the enemy. 1
When caught in the mountains, rely on their valleys.
Position yourself on the heights facing the sun.
To win your battles, never attack uphill.
This is how you position your army in the mountains.

⁶When water blocks you, keep far away from it.
Let the invader cross the river and wait for him.
Do not meet him in midstream.
Wait for him to get half his forces across and
then take advantage of the situation.

¹⁰You need to be able to fight.
You can't do that if you are caught in water
when you meet an invader.
Position yourself upstream, facing the sun.
Never face against the current.
Always position your army upstream when
near the water.

FOUR:

The number **four**
卩丩 *represents
the connected
ideas of four
external com-
pass points and
the four steps
used to advance
a position.*

The Path of Progress

1 Warriors make progress by outmaneuvering their opponents.
When the playing field is uneven, follow the path of least resistance.
Strategy requires that you use the unevenness of the ground.
You never meet opponents when they control the high ground.
You can make progress by using the inequities of the ground.

When change is an obstacle, avoid it entirely.
When others try a difficult transition, be patient.
You should never join them.
You want to engage others in the middle of a transition and look for opportunities.

MARCH:

You must overcome challenges.
You cannot fight the trends and deal with your challenges at the same time.
You must use the pressure of change in your favor.
Use the trends instead of fighting them.
Your progress depends on getting the forces of change on your side.

This is the first of the three longest and most complex chapters. These chapters explore all the details that make every situation unique.

¹⁵You may have to move across marshes.
Move through them quickly without stopping.
You may meet the enemy in the middle of a marsh.
You must keep on the water grasses.
Keep your back to a clump of trees.
This is how you position your army in a marsh.

²¹On a level plateau, take a position that you can change.
Keep the higher ground on your right and to the rear.
Keep danger in front of you and safety behind.
This is how you position yourself on a level plateau.

²⁵You can find an advantage in all four of these situations.
Learn from the great emperor who used positioning to conquer his four rivals.

Armies are stronger on high ground and weaker on low. 2
They are better camping on sunny southern hillsides than
on shady northern ones.
Provide for your army's health and place men correctly.
Your army will be free from disease.
Done correctly, this means victory.

⁶You must sometimes defend on a hill or riverbank.
You must keep on the south side in the sun.
Keep the uphill slope at your right rear.

⁹This will give the advantage to your army.
It will always give you a position of strength.

Sometimes you must get through an uncertain situation.
You must get through these times without getting bogged down.
People can move against you when your situation is unclear.
All you can do is stick to what you know.
You must avoid getting pushed into a worse mess.
You must make progress even when your situation is unclear.

When all things are equal, you want to keep your options open.
You must use every advantage of your position.
Face your opponents directly but keep a fallback position.
You can make good progress on an equal playing field.

You can find opportunities in every situation you face.
Warriors master the techniques necessary to overcome opponents
under any conditions.

2 Warriors know how to recognize the ethical high ground.
People are more vigorous working out in the open than they are
working secretly.
Principled, honorable positions strengthen your support.
Corrupt, dishonest positions make people cynical.
Ethical behavior translates to long-term success.

Sometimes you are forced to defend a questionable position.
You can still be honest about your situation.
You need strong support behind you.

Strong principles create opportunities.
Principles also create unity, which is the source of strength.

Stop the march when the rain swells the river into rapids. 3
You may want to ford the river.
Wait until it subsides.

4All regions can have seasonal mountain streams that can
cut you off.
There are seasonal lakes.
There are seasonal blockages.
There are seasonal jungles.
There are seasonal floods.
There are seasonal fissures.
Get away from all these quickly.
Do not get close to them.
Keep them at a distance.
Maneuver the enemy close to them.
Position yourself facing these dangers.
Push the enemy back into them.

16Danger can hide on your army's flank.
There are reservoirs and lakes.
There are reeds and thickets.
There are mountain woods.
Their dense vegetation provides a hiding place.
You must cautiously search through them.
They can always hide an ambush.

HEAVEN:

The concept of **heaven** 天 *indicates the natural cycle of changes in the environment that cannot be controlled but can be predicted.*

3 Warriors stop before being overwhelmed by sudden changes.
You must navigate change.
This requires patience.

The changing climate is continually reshaping your situation, creating obstacles.
There temporary unknowns.
There are temporary blockages.
There are temporary maze
There are temporary pressures.
There are temporary traps.
Use speed to avoid these obstacles.
The sooner you react the better.
Keep away from these shifting sands.
Let others pursue short-lived novelties.
Watch what happens to them.
Encourage other to test the ground.

Not all dangers are readily apparent.
There are dangers in change.
There are dangers in growth.
There are dangers in growing inequity.
You have to be wary of hidden threats.
Trust your suspicions.
You cannot afford to be blindsided.

METAPHORS:

All of these lessons can be connected metaphorically to competitive situations in your personal and business life.

Sometimes, the enemy is close by but remains calm. 4
Expect to find him in a natural stronghold.
Other times he remains at a distance but provokes battle.
He wants you to attack him.

5He sometimes shifts the position of his camp.
He is looking for an advantageous position.

7The trees in the forest move.
Expect that the enemy is coming.
The tall grasses obstruct your view.
Be suspicious.

11The birds take flight.
Expect that the enemy is hiding.
Animals startle.
Expect an ambush.

15Notice the dust.
It sometimes rises high in a straight line.
Vehicles are coming.
The dust appears low in a wide band.
Foot soldiers are coming.
The dust seems scattered in different areas.
The enemy is collecting firewood.
Any dust is light and settling down.
The enemy is setting up camp.

PLACE:

The ground is the place 所 of battle, but the nature of place is determined by changes over time under the control of heaven.

4 Warriors know how to interpret the actions of others.
When people are confident, they have a secret advantage.
Even those far away can still act in a threatening manner.
They don't invite attack without a reason.

People do not normally move from where they are comfortable.
They move only to pursue opportunities.

Notice the changes in establish systems.
Expect that a new challenge is coming.
Be wary when you can't see what is happening.
You cannot be too careful.

Sensitive people sense changes first.
Expect a hidden challenge.
People can appear nervous.
Expect to be surprised.

Every action leaves some small sign.
These signs can be obvious and straightforward.
This indicates others moving very quickly.
Signs can be subtle and broad.
This indicates others moving very broadly.
Signs can pop up here and there.
This indicates others slowing down.
Signs can be spotty and declining.
This indicates others pausing.

ADAPTATION:

Our many adaptations of Sun Tzu's work explain how you can apply these analogies and ideas to common competitive situations.

Your enemy speaks humbly while building up forces. 5
He is planning to advance.

3The enemy talks aggressively and pushes as if to advance.
He is planning to retreat.

5Small vehicles exit his camp first.
They move the army's flanks.
They are forming a battle line.

8Your enemy tries to sue for peace but without offering a
treaty.
He is plotting.

10Your enemy's men run to leave and yet form ranks.
You should expect action.

12Half his army advances and the other half retreats.
He is luring you.

14Your enemy plans to fight but his men just stand there.
They are starving.

16Those who draw water drink it first.
They are thirsty.

18Your enemy sees an advantage but does not advance.
His men are tired.

5 Warriors notice when people's words differ from their actions.
An opponent is trying to mislead you.

You need not fear the most aggressive behavior.
It is often a smoke screen for weakness.

Notice when people suddenly change in subtle ways.
Notice when they defend themselves too quickly.
They want to pick a fight.

Anyone can say that they want peace, but they are not serious if
they reject compromises that permit peace.
Peace can be just a trick.

When people are afraid of you, they befriend each other.
They can unite against you.

Distrust obvious openings when facing a challenge.
Do let it tempt you into acting rashly.

When a rival's supporters do nothing, there is always a reason.
They lack resources.

Individuals in groups can act in their personal self-interest.
They no longer trust their organization.

Your opponents may fail to seize an obvious opportunity.
Their resources are exhausted.

²⁰Birds gather.
Your enemy has abandoned his camp.

²²Your enemy's soldiers call in the night.
They are afraid.

²⁴Your enemy's army is raucous.
The men do not take their commander seriously.

²⁶Your enemy's banners and flags shift.
Order is breaking down.

²⁸Your enemy's officers are irritable.
They are exhausted.

³⁰Your enemy's men kill their horses for meat.
They are out of provisions.

³²They don't put their pots away or return to their tents.
They are desperate.

³⁴Enemy troops appear sincere and agreeable.
But their men are slow to speak to each other.
They are no longer united.

³⁷Your enemy offers too many incentives to his men.
He is in trouble.

³⁹Your enemy gives out too many punishments.
His men are weary.

Scavengers can be informative.
When people move on, scavengers follow behind.

A group of people shows their emotions.
Their fear is contagious.

Any group can react wildly.
It means the members have lost confidence in their leader.

Reorganization is another sign of weakness.
It indicates a breakdown of unity and focus.

Poor decisions are made in anger.
Weariness is the source of most anger.

Only desperate people sacrifice their mobility.
Only survival is more important.

Some people are indifferent to self-preservation.
These people are dangerous.

Communication is the key to coordination.
Friends can be reluctant to share information.
Their friendship is weak.

People shouldn't have to bribe their supporters.
This is a sign of discord.

People also shouldn't punish their supporters.
This is a sign of laziness.

⁴¹Your enemy first acts violently and then is afraid of your
larger force.
His best troops have not arrived.

⁴³Your enemy comes in a conciliatory manner.
He needs to rest and recuperate.

⁴⁵Your enemy is angry and appears to welcome battle.
This goes on for a long time, but he doesn't attack.
He also doesn't leave the field.
You must watch him carefully.

If you are too weak to fight, you must find more men. 6
In this situation, you must not act aggressively.
You must unite your forces.
Prepare for the enemy.
Recruit men and stay where you are.

⁶You must be cautious about making plans and adjust to the
enemy.
You must gather more men.

CAUTION:

The proper reaction to ignorance is **caution** 謹*, which requires edging into situations incrementally, being skeptical about appearances.*

Opponents can attack before they are ready, to throw us off balance and delay our progress.

They may expect additional support soon.

Opponents can suddenly pretend that they to want to be friends.
This can also be a delaying tactic.

Sometimes your rivals' behavior is just confusing.
They don't know if they want to confront you or not.
They won't leave you alone.
Your vigilance is your best defense against them.

6 When your progress stalls, you need more resources.
You must not challenge your opposition.
You must gather your resources.
Prepare to defend yourself.
Build up support where you are.

Plan on defending yourself and keep track of what opponents are doing.
You must buy time to build up your resources.

MASTERY:

Remember-ing all these details would be impossible if they weren't connected to an underlying system that you can master.

With new, undedicated soldiers, you can depend on them 7
if you discipline them.
They will tend to disobey your orders.
If they do not obey your orders, they will be useless.

4You can depend on seasoned, dedicated soldiers.
But you must avoid disciplining them without reason.
Otherwise, you cannot use them.

7You must control your soldiers with esprit de
corps.
You must bring them together by winning
victories.
You must get them to believe in you.

10Make it easy for people to know what to do
by training your people.
Your people will then obey you.
If you do not make it easy for people to
know what to do, you won't train your
people.
Then they will not obey.

14Make your commands easy to follow.
You must understand the way a crowd thinks.

♦ ♦ ♦

COMMAND:

The concept of **command** 令 *is defined specifically as giving instructions of how a group of people must move*—**march** 行—*connecting a leader to his or her followers.*

7 Warriors use discipline because they must train their apprentices to be dependable.

Novices lack good judgment.

To be productive, you begin by following orders.

When you develop experience, you become dependable.

You need neither direction nor punishment to do what is needed.

This makes you valuable.

You must give your team mates a good feeling about our team.

When people share successes, their friendships are solidified.

PEOPLE:

Trust is the foundation of all teams.

You train other people by making it easy for other people to know what to do and why.

This is the key to leadership.

If you send mixed messages about what is needed and why, others cannot know how you want them to act.

They also lose faith in you.

Strategy only works because humans are more predictable and controllable than events. If you think you can be successful alone, you need more training.

Keep what you say straightforward and simple.

Know how people can misinterpret what you say.

♦ ♦ ♦

Related Articles from *Sun Tzu's Playbook*

In chapter nine, Sun Tzu discusses the basics of recognizing conditions in new territory. To learn the step-by-step techniques involved, we recommend the Sun Tzu's Art of War Playbook *articles listed below.*

1.1.0 Position Paths: the continuity of strategic positions over time.

1.2.2 Exploiting Exploration: how competitive landscapes are searched and positions utilized.

2.1 Information Value: knowledge and communication as the basis of strategy.

2.1.1 Information Limits: making good decisions with limited information.

2.2.1 Personal Relationships: why information depends on personal relationships.

2.2.2 Mental Models: how mental models simplify decision-making.

2.2.3 Standard Terminology: how mental models must be shared to enable communication.

2.3 Personal Interactions: making progress through personal interactions.

2.3.1 Action and Reaction: how we advance based on how others react to our actions.

2.3.2 Reaction Unpredictability: why we can never exactly predict the reactions of others.

2.3.3 Likely Reactions: the range of potential reactions in gathering information.

2.3.4 Using Questions: using questions in gathering information and predicting reactions.

4.0 Leveraging Probability: making better decisions regarding our choice of opportunities.

4.3 Leveraging Form: how we can leverage the form of our territory.

4.3.1 Tilted Forms: opportunities that are dominated by uneven forces.

4.3.2 Fluid Forms: opportunities that are dominated by fast-changing directional forces.

4.3.3 Soft Forms: opportunities that are dominated by forces that create uncertainty.

4.3.4 Neutral Forms: opportunities where the terrain has no dominant forces.

4.4 Strategic Distance: relative proximity in strategic space.

4.4.1 Physical Distance: the issues of proximity in physical space.

4.4.2 Intellectual Distance: the challenges of moving through intellectual space.

Chapter 10

地 形

Field Position: The Vision of Opportunity

Everyone holds a number of different positions in life. At school, at work, and even in our personal lives, our roles are always changing. Warriors think of every position that they hold as a stepping-stone to future success. Each role in life represents a special type of opportunity. Each position has its own advantages and disadvantages. Your current role and abilities reveal your next opportunity.

Not all positions are the same. Warriors know how to make the right moves so that each step makes the step after that easier. Strategy provides a simple method for weighing your opportunities so you can make the right choices. After awhile, you will instantly see where each choice will naturally lead.

The vision you follow is largely a matter of your character. Warriors are sensitive to the personal flaws that handicap regular people. Warriors work to eliminate these flaws in themselves while they work to exploit these flaws in others.

Warriors do not make choices to satisfy other people's expectations. You are the only person in a position to choose the right course for you. Warriors do not make their choices based upon a desire to win praise or avoid criticism.

Warriors recognize their responsibility to their loved ones. They recognize that they must act as leaders and role models. Giving people what they need is more important than giving them what they want. To choose the right path in life is a matter of being objective about your obstacles, capabilities, and principles.

Field Position

SIX:

The number
six 六 *arises*
naturally from
the three sets of
opposites that
define the three
physical dimen-
sions of the
ground.

SUN TZU SAID:

Some field positions are unobstructed. 1
Some field positions are entangling.
Some field positions are supporting.
Some field positions are constricted.
Some field positions give you a barricade.
Some field positions are spread out.

⁷You can attack from some positions easily.
Other forces can meet you easily as well.
We call these unobstructed positions.
These positions are open.
On them, be the first to occupy a high, sunny
area.
Put yourself where you can defend your
supply routes.
Then you will have an advantage.

The Vision of Opportunity

1 Warriors recognize when their roles are wide open.
They recognize roles that cannot be recaptured.
They recognize roles that last a lifetime.
They recognize roles that are controlling.
They recognize roles that protect them.
They recognize roles that are too diluted.

Some roles offer you many ways to move forward.
Your rivals can easily challenge any of your moves.
These roles are wide open opportunities.
They are open to you and to your opponents as well.
You must use speed to get the benefit of them as
stepping-stones.
As you move forward, consider your long-term
needs.
These roles offer the easiest path to the future.

DEFINITIONS:

*The chapter be-
gins with more
definitions.
These defini-
tions are hard
to remember
unless you learn
their pattern.*

DISASTER:

*Sun Tzu uses the term **disaster** 難 to indicate the degradation of a position to the point where it becomes untenable and cannot support you or be defended.*

[14]You can attack from some positions easily.
Disaster arises when you try to return to them.
These are entangling positions.
These field positions are one-sided.
Wait until your enemy is unprepared.
You can then attack from these positions and win.
Avoid a well-prepared enemy.
You will try to attack and lose.
Since you can't return, you will meet disaster.
These field positions offer no advantage.

[24]You cannot leave some positions without losing an advantage.
If the enemy leaves this ground, he also loses an advantage.
We call these supporting field positions.
These positions strengthen you.
The enemy may try to entice you away.
Still, hold your position.
You must entice the enemy to leave.
You then strike him as he is leaving.
These field positions offer an advantage.

[33]Some field positions are constricted.
Get to these positions first.
You must fill these areas and await the enemy.
Sometimes, the enemy will reach them first.
If he fills them, do not follow him.
However, if he fails to fill them, you can go after him.

Some roles offer opportunities to move forward.
If you leave these rolls, you will never be invited
back into them.
You cannot return to them.
They are like a one-way street.
If patient, you can these roles as stepping-stones.
You must be certain your next opportunity is solid
before moving on.
You cannot make the wrong move.
If you fail to move forward, your position is worse.
These roles offer you no fallback position.
These roles are not the most beneficial.

*The power
of mastering
strategy is that
it gives you the
tools to recog-
nize common
situations and
know instantly
how to react.*

Some roles are perfect opportunities that no similar position can
improve upon.
No one who attains these positions can afford to leave them.
You want these roles to last a lifetime.
The advantage they offer never diminishes.
Everyone will try to tempt you out of these roles.
You must appreciate how rare these situations are.
Let other people take them for granted.
When others abandon these roles, move instantly.
These positions are well worth controlling.

Some roles are exclusive.
The first person to win them can take control.
If you attain these positions first, you can stop rivals behind you.
If other people reach these positions first, observe how they behave.
If they bar your progress, do not challenge them.
If they do not block you, you can follow behind them.

³⁹Some field positions give you a barricade.
Get to these positions first.
You must occupy their southern, sunny heights in order to
await the enemy.
Sometimes the enemy occupies these areas first.
If so, entice him away.
Never go after him.

⁴⁵Some field positions are too spread out.
Your force may seem equal to the enemy.
Still you will lose if you provoke a battle.
If you fight, you will not have any advantage.

⁴⁹These are the six types of field positions.
Each battleground has its own rules.
As a commander, you must know where to go.
You must examine each position closely.

Some armies can be outmaneuvered. 2
Some armies are too lax.
Some armies fall down.
Some armies fall apart.
Some armies are disorganized.
Some armies must retreat.

⁷Know all six of these weaknesses.
They create weak timing and disastrous posi-
tions.
They all arise from the army's commander.

SUBJECT:

The character
者 *is usually
translated as
is but it is not
the verb **to be**.
Instead it is used
to indicate the
subject under
the discussion.*

Some roles can protect you.

You want to get into these roles quickly.

These roles give you authority and visibility that is easy to use if you are patient.

You must recognize when your opponents are in these roles.

Your rivals are protected by these roles.

You cannot attack them directly.

Some roles are too diluted.

These positions undermine your strength.

When you fall into these roles, you are weak compared with others.

These roles make it difficult to meet a challenge.

You must recognize the abstract forms of these six roles.

Every real role combines their qualities to some degree.

As a warrior, you have a choice about what roles you play.

You must understand the underlying nature of your opportunity.

2 Warriors recognize confusion.

They recognize laziness.

They recognize a lack of training.

They recognize insecurity.

They recognize self-indulgence.

They recognize a lack of foresight.

You must recognize weaknesses in people.

These weaknesses make progress impossible past a certain point.

They are simply character flaws.

TRAINING:

Our Warrior Class on-line training teaches the "warrior mind" so that you can recognize common situations and respond instinctively.

¹⁰One general can command a force equal to the enemy.
Still his enemy outflanks him.
This means that his army can be outmaneuvered.

¹³Another can have strong soldiers but weak officers.
This means that his army is too lax.

¹⁵Another has strong officers but weak soldiers.
This means that his army will fall down.

¹⁷Another has subcommanders who are angry and defiant.
They attack the enemy and fight their own battles.
The commander cannot know the battlefield.
This means that his army will fall apart.

²¹Another general is weak and easygoing.
He fails to make his orders clear.
His officers and men lack direction.
This shows in his military formations.
This means that his army is disorganized.

GENERAL:

The concept **general** 將 *means both the commander and a commander's activities, that is, making decisions and giving commands.*

²⁶Another general fails to predict the enemy.
He pits his small forces against larger ones.
His weak forces attack stronger ones.
He fails to pick his fights correctly.
This means that his army must retreat.

Some people start with every advantage in life.
Still, others consistently outperform them.
These people are confused.

Some people have good skills but lack drive.
These people are too lazy.

Some people have drive but lack good skills.
These people are untrained.

Some people are easily upset and confrontational.
They attack others and are always defending themselves.
They lose track of what their goals are.
These people are insecure.

Some people are indecisive and carefree.
They never identify their goals.
Their drive and skills lack any focus.
They take new positions on any whim.
These people are self-indulgent.

EQUATIONS:

These definitions are like mathematical equations of interconnecting ideas that anyone can master if given the proper training.

Some people never think about their future.
They invest too little effort into long-term gains.
They spend more than they earn.
They are always coming up short.
These people are short-sighted.

³¹You must know all about these six weaknesses.
You must understand the philosophies that lead to defeat.
When a general arrives, you can know what he will do.
You must study each general carefully.

You must control your field position. 3
It will always strengthen your army.

³You must predict the enemy to overpower him and win.
You must analyze the obstacles, dangers, and distances.
This is the best way to command.

⁶Understand your field position before you go to battle.
Then you will win.
You can fail to understand your field position and still fight.
Then you will lose.

¹⁰You must provoke battle when you will certainly win.
It doesn't matter what you are ordered.
The government may order you not to fight.
Despite that, you must always fight when you
will win.

¹⁴Sometimes provoking a battle will lead to a
loss.
The government may order you to fight.
Despite that, you must avoid battle when you
will lose.

RULER:

The **ruler** 主
*means manag-
ing the produc-
tive resources
of a nation, as a*
general 將 *man-
ages its compet-
itive resources.*

You must instantly see through these character flaws.
Certain world views lead to these weaknesses.
People with these flaws are very predictable.
You must analyze yourself and others.

3 A warrior uses every opportunity as a stepping-stone.
Each step must improve your position.

You must foresee how you can meet opposition and still succeed.
Choose your path by considering the problems it might lead to.
Everything depends on making the right decisions.

You must examine your options before you accept any challenge.
You will naturally choose the easiest path.
Unfortunately, most people seldom look before they leap.
This is why they so often fail.

You must accept every challenge that leads to success.
You do not need to do what everyone expects.
People are controlled by the expectations of others.
Warriors are dedicated to constant progress
toward better positions.

You must avoid every challenge that leads to
failure.
Do get pressured into undertaking them.
You cannot waste your time on paths that take you
nowhere.

PRINCIPLES:

*We developed
the Science
of Strategy
Institute as a
resource to help
make learning
these principles
easy, interest-
ing, and fun.*

[17]You must advance without desiring praise.
You must retreat without fearing shame.
The only correct move is to preserve your troops.
This is how you serve your country.
This is how you reward your nation.

Think of your soldiers as little children. 4
You can make them follow you into a deep river.
Treat them as your beloved children.
You can lead them all to their deaths.

[5]Some leaders are generous but cannot use their men.
They love their men but cannot command them.
Their men are unruly and disorganized.
These leaders create spoiled children.
Their soldiers are useless.

You may know what your soldiers will do in an attack. 5
You may not know if the enemy is vulnerable to attack.
You will then win only half the time.
You may know that the enemy is vulnerable to attack.
You may not know if your men have the capability of attacking him.
You will still win only half the time.
You may know that the enemy is vulnerable to attack.
You may know that your men are ready to attack.
You may not, however, know how to position yourself in the field for battle.
You will still win only half the time.

You must put aside your desire for praise.
You must put aside your fear of failure.
You must use your limited resources in the best possible way.
This is the only way you really satisfy others.
This is how you do your duty.

4 Warriors recognize their influence over friends and family.
You must take responsibility for the people you love.
You must accept your responsibility.
You must recognize your power to affect their lives.

Regular people think they should give everyone what they want.
They supply affection when people really need direction.
This makes people unhappy and confused.
Pampering people destroys their ability to make decisions.
This results in tragedy.

5 Warriors know exactly how their abilities help them advance.
Regular people forget to think about the obstacles in their path.
This is why failure is so common.
You can know exactly how to overcome the obstacles in your path.
You still must have the abilities and resources needed to meet those
challenges at hand.
Without preparation, success is a coin flip.
You can know exactly how to overcome the obstacles in your path.
You can have the abilities and resources to meet those challenges.
You must also know how to select each opportunity as a stepping-
stone to future success.
You do not want to fail because you chose the wrong path.

[11]You must know how to make war.
You can then act without confusion.
You can attempt anything.

[14]We say:
Know the enemy and know yourself.
Your victory will be painless.
Know the weather and the field.
Your victory will be complete.

✦ ✦ ✦

CONFUSION:

The concept of **confusion** 迷 *indicates both a lack of clear direction and a lack of consistency. By definition, an action cannot go in two opposing directions at once.*

You must see your path clearly.
You work toward success one step at a time.
No eventual goal is too large.

Warriors know the truth.
You match your skills to the obstacles before you.
Success will come easily.
Use the trends and your opportunities.
There is no limit to your success.

COMPLETION:

Everyone tries to use strategy, but only those skilled in its methods are successful. A single missing piece prevents you from completing a puzzle.

Related Articles from *Sun Tzu's Playbook*

In chapter ten, Sun Tzu discusses the use of temporary positions in building relationships with voters. To learn the step-by-step techniques involved, we recommend the Sun Tzu's Art of War Playbook *articles listed below.*

2.3 Personal Interactions: making progress through personal interactions.

2.3.1 Action and Reaction: how we advance based on how others reaction to our actions.

2.3.2 Reaction Unpredictability: why we can never exactly predict the react of others.

2.3.3 Likely Reactions: the range of potential reactions in gathering information.

2.3.4 Using Questions: using questions in gathering information and predicting reactions.

4.5 Opportunity Surfaces: judging potential opportunities from a distance.

4.5.1 Surface Area: choosing opportunities on the basis of their size.

4.5.2 Surface Barriers: how to select opportunities by evaluating obstacles.

4.5.3 Surface Holding Power: sticky and slippery situations.

4.6 Six Benchmarks: simplifying the comparisons of opportunities.

4.6.1 Spread-Out Conditions: recognizing opportunities that are too large.

4.6.2 Constricted Conditions: identifying and using constricted positions.

4.6.3 Barricaded Conditions: the issues related to the extremes of obstacles.

4.6.4 Wide-Open Conditions: the issues related to an absence of barriers.

4.6.5 Fixed Conditions: positions with extreme holding power.

4.6.6 Sensitive Conditions: positions with no holding power on pursuing opportunities.

4.7 Competitive Weakness: how certain opportunities can bring out our weaknesses.

4.7.1 Command Weaknesses: the character flaws of leaders and how to exploit them.

4.7.2 Group Weaknesses: organizational weakness and where groups fail.

4.8 Climate Support: choosing new positions based on future changes.

4.9 Opportunity Mapping: two-dimensional tool for comparing opportunity probabilities.

Chapter 11

九地

Types of Terrain: The Miracle of Training

Becoming a warrior requires developing a warrior's mind. The warrior's mind is trained in perception and decision-making. The warrior's mind sees the key relationships that define a situation and reacts instantly based on training.

To know how to respond, you don't have to know how to sort through thousands, hundreds, or even dozens of different situations. Sun Tzu defines only nine basic situations that require a specific form of response. Warriors can act instantly and confidently based on their recognition of these situations.

Strategy is a process of continually leveraging your opportunities. You must always expand your capabilities. When you commit yourself to continual progress, you must also commit yourself to refining your decision-making skills.

When you are confident in your decisions, you are committed to a course of action. Warriors appreciate the power of commitment. When you are truly committed, you no longer waste your efforts preparing for failure. After a commitment is made, the most important quality is your speed of response. A warrior's responses are a trained reflex.

Trained decision-makers are natural leaders. You can accomplish little alone. You need the support of others to be successful. Good leadership requires identifying the best challenges to tackle. New challenges hold a team together and keep it moving forward.

Types of Terrain

GROUND:

The concept of ground 地 *also means* terrain, situation, *and* condition, *which is why it is used to describe so many aspects of a position.*

SUN TZU SAID:

Use the art of war. 1
Know when the terrain will scatter you.
Know when the terrain will be easy.
Know when the terrain will be disputed.
Know when the terrain is open.
Know when the terrain is intersecting.
Know when the terrain is dangerous.
Know when the terrain is bad.
Know when the terrain is confined.
Know when the terrain is deadly.

[11]Warring parties must sometimes fight inside their own territory.
This is scattering terrain.

[13]When you enter hostile territory, your penetration is shallow.
This is easy terrain.

[15]Some terrain gives you an advantageous position.
But it gives others an advantageous position as well.
This will be disputed terrain.

The Miracle of Training

THE WARRIOR HEARS:

1 Warriors the ability to choose.
You must see circumstances can divide people.
You must recognize simple challenges.
You must recognize sources of conflict.
You must recognize when you have few obstacles.
You must see when to bring people together.
You must recognize difficult challenges.
You must recognize when progress will be difficult.
You must recognize when you are vulnerable.
You must recognize when you are desperate.

This chapter describes both conditions on the ground and situations that arise over time as you advance your position.

Learn what happens when people are threatened
where they once felt safe.
Their unity dissolves.

Learn to expect a honeymoon period in a new project or campaign.
Your progress seems so simple.

Learn that areas that are too desirable create conflict.
If you want to win these rewards, so will many others.
These situations are sources of conflict.

[18]You can use some terrain to advance easily.
Others can advance along with you.
This is open terrain.

[21]Everyone shares access to a given area.
The first one to arrive there can gather a larger group than anyone else.
This is intersecting terrain.

[24]You can penetrate deeply into hostile territory.
Then many hostile cities are behind you.
This is dangerous terrain.

[27]There are mountain forests.
There are dangerous obstructions.
There are reservoirs.
Everyone confronts these obstacles on a campaign.
They make bad terrain.

[32]In some areas, the entry passage is narrow.
You are closed in as you try to get out of them.
In this type of area, a few people can effectively attack your much larger force.
This is confined terrain.

[36]You can sometimes survive only if you fight quickly.
You will die if you delay.
This is deadly terrain.

Learn what happens when you are making quick progress.
Everyone else is probably making good progress as well.
These situations have few real obstacles.

Learn about areas in which people's interests naturally come together.
Use these areas to aggressively build a team and organize team-
mates for a shared goal.
Use the circumstances to bring people together.

Learn that a project or campaign changes as time goes on.
The more progress you make, the more resistance you encounter.
These challenges are increasingly difficult.

Learn when you must work your way through problems.
You must be very careful of some situations.
You must work your way around some obstacles.
You never make progress without encountering problems.
These situations slow down your progress.

Learn to recognize critical transition points.
These situations limit what you can do.
You are dependent on others and defenseless against attack in these
situations.
Critical transitions make you vulnerable.

Learn when you must react instantly to a challenge.
Wasting even a minute can be fatal.
You are truly desperate.

³⁹To be successful, you must control scattering terrain by avoiding battle.

Control easy terrain by not stopping.

Control disputed terrain by not attacking.

Control open terrain by staying with the enemy's forces.

Control intersecting terrain by uniting with your allies.

Control dangerous terrain by plundering.

Control bad terrain by keeping on the move.

Control confined terrain by using surprise.

Control deadly terrain by fighting.

Go to an area that is known to be good for waging war. 2

Use it to cut off the enemy's contact between his front and back lines.

Prevent his small parties from relying on his larger force.

Stop his strong divisions from rescuing his weak ones.

Prevent his officers from getting their men together.

Chase his soldiers apart to stop them from amassing.

Harass them to prevent their ranks from forming.

DEATH:

The concept translated as **death** 死 *also means* **deadly, desperate, to kill,** *and* **final.** *It is the final stage in all cam- paigns.*

⁸When joining battle gives you an advantage, you must do it.

When it isn't to your benefit, you must avoid it.

¹⁰A daring soldier may ask:
"A large, organized enemy army and its gen- eral are coming.
What do I do to prepare for them?"

Since a challenge in your own area is divisive, success depends on moving into new areas.

Success depends on getting the most out of your initial progress.

Success depends on avoiding prizes everyone is fighting for.

Success depends on speed when there are few obstacles.

Success depends on finding opportunities to build alliances.

Success depends on getting rewarded for expensive projects.

Success depends on working through every obstacle.

Success depends on keeping your vulnerabilities a secret.

Success depends on fighting only when you are desperate.

2 Warriors train to identify situations that offer opportunities. These situations offer you an opening that allows you to divide and conquer.

You can win small victories in the face of serious challenges.

You can avoid serious opposition while solving minor problems.

You stop little problems from becoming more serious.

You make quick progress to prevent opposition from growing.

Your progress makes it difficult for critics to attack you.

When meeting a challenge creates such opportunities, meet it.

When a challenge offers you no such opportunities, avoid it.

Warriors must ask brave questions.

It is sometimes obvious when you are going to be attacked.

You must know how to defend yourself.

TEXT BLOCKS:

Each new block of text (indicated by the large numbers) describes each "terrain" in more detail. The text assumes the context.

¹³Tell him:

"First seize an area that the enemy must have.
Then he will pay attention to you.
Mastering speed is the essence of war.
Take advantage of a large enemy's inability to keep up.
Use a philosophy of avoiding difficult situations.
Attack the area where he doesn't expect you."

You must use the philosophy of an invader. 3
Invade deeply and then concentrate your forces.
This controls your men without oppressing them.

⁴Get your supplies from the riches of the territory.
They are sufficient to supply your whole army.

⁶Take care of your men and do not overtax them.
Your esprit de corps increases your momentum.
Keep your army moving and plan for surprises.
Make it difficult for the enemy to count your forces.
Position your men where there is no place to run.
They will then face death without fleeing.
They will find a way to survive.
Your officers and men will fight to their utmost.

¹⁴Military officers who are committed lose their fear.
When they have nowhere to run, they must stand firm.
Deep in enemy territory, they are captives.
Since they cannot escape, they will fight.

Your reaction is simple.
Instead of defending yourself, look for your opponent's weakness.
By targeting a weakness, you shift your opponent's focus.
Speed is important because it gives you the initiative.
If you maintain the initiative, opponents don't know where to turn.
You avoid fighting in your own territory, even to defend yourself.
You must move the battle where your opponent doesn't want it.

3 Warriors are trained to use the power of commitment.
When people are deeply committed, they develop better focus.
Commitment maintains a team's focus without creating divisions.

Being committed to conquering a new area is always rewarding.
New challenges stimulate everyone.

Take care of your teammates and don't push them too hard.
Nurture a sense of team spirit to keep everyone united.
You maintain your momentum by preparing for things to go wrong.
You want your opponents to underestimate you.
You want solid commitments from your teammates.
Once people are committed, they cannot back down.
You will learn what you need to do to succeed.
Working together gets the best efforts out of everyone.

When you make a commitment, your uncertainty vanishes.
Once you choose a course of action, you must stay with it.
The more opposition you overcome, the stronger you become.
You must not leave yourself an easy way to back out.

[18]Commit your men completely.
Without being posted, they will be on guard.
Without being asked, they will get what is needed.
Without being forced, they will be dedicated.
Without being given orders, they can be trusted.

[23]Stop them from guessing by removing all their doubts.
Stop them from dying by giving them no place to run.

[25]Your officers may not be rich.
Nevertheless, they still desire plunder.
They may die young.
Nevertheless, they still want to live forever.

[29]You must order the time of attack.
Officers and men may sit and weep until their lapels are wet.
When they stand up, tears may stream down their cheeks.
Put them in a position where they cannot run.
They will show the greatest courage under fire.

SNAKE:

The use of the term **snake** 蛇 *is an analogy for an army on the march on a long trail and for the twisting path of the campaign itself.*

Make good use of war. 4
This demands instant reflexes.
You must develop these instant reflexes.
Act like an ordinary mountain snake.
If people strike your head then stop them
with your tail.
If they strike your tail then stop them with
your head.
If they strike your middle then use both your
head and tail.

Choose teammates who are devoted.
You want them to share your sense of responsibility.
Their judgment can be as valuable as your own.
People shouldn't have to be nagged to do what is needed.
You must be able to trust your teammates' devotion.

You must stop second-guessing yourself to be confident.
Your success is more certain when you stop looking for excuses.

People are motivated by self-interest.
Everyone wants greater success.
People are willing to take risks.
This doesn't mean that they don't value what they have.

The time comes when everyone must act.
People will argue and complain until that time comes.
Even when the time comes, they will still complain.
Once people make a commitment, they cannot back down.
People show incredible courage when they commit themselves.

4 Warriors train to react quickly.
You must respond instantly to any situation.
Train yourself to recognize these nine situations.
Your responses should be instinctual.
People challenge your thoughts, force them to think about your feelings.
People challenge your feeling, give them a feel for you ideas.
If they challenge your personally, challenge them to talk about thoughts and feelings

DETAIL:

The point of these three long chapters is that when you diagnose your situation, you know instantly how to react appropriately.

[8]A daring soldier asks:
"Can any army imitate these instant reflexes?"
We answer:
"It can."

[12]To command and get the most out of proud people, you
must study adversity.
People work together when they are in the same boat during
a storm.
In this situation, one rescues the other just as the right
hand helps the left.

[15]Use adversity correctly.
Tether your horses and bury your wagon's wheels.
Still, you can't depend on this alone.
An organized force is braver than lone individuals.
This is the art of organization.
Put the tough and weak together.
You must also use the terrain.

[22]Make good use of war.
Unite your men as one.
Never let them give up.

The commander must be a military professional. 5
This requires confidence and detachment.
You must maintain dignity and order.
You must control what your men see and hear.
They must follow you without knowing your plans.

Is speed always possible?
Can a group of people always know how to work together?
Your training is the key.
You must train as a team.

Sharing a common enemy and common dangers draws people together.
The more teammates have to lose, the most smoothly they work together.
When the threat is big enough, people don't think twice about helping one another.

A threatening situation can work for you.
You can tell yourself that you are totally committed to your course.
Your individual commitment alone will not save you.
When others are depending on you, you forget your personal fears.
This the real power of teamwork.
The range of a team's abilities overcomes its flaws.
You must use your situation.

Strategy is the key to success.
Unity is the source of strength.
Persistence assures your success.

5 Warriors train in the art of leadership.
You must demonstrate self-assurance and objectivity.
Teammates must respect your seriousness and your priorities.
Always pay attention to the impression you are creating.
People must have faith in the decisions that you make.

6You can reinvent your men's roles.

You can change your plans.

You can use your men without their understanding.

9You must shift your campgrounds.

You must take detours from the ordinary routes.

You must use men without telling them about your strategy.

12A commander provides what is needed now.

This is like climbing high and being willing to kick away your ladder.

You must be able to lead your men deep into different surrounding territory.

And yet, you can discover the opportunity to win.

16You must drive men like a flock of sheep.

You must drive them to march.

You must drive them to attack.

You must never let them know where you are headed.

You must unite them into a great army.

You must then drive them against all opposition.

This is the job of a true commander.

23You must adapt to the different terrain.

You must adapt to find an advantage.

You must manage your people's affections.

You must study all these skills.

You must see the possibilities in everyone.

Your goals must always evolve.

You can get more out of people than they know they have to give.

You can break teammates of their old habits.

You can lead them to places they never expected to go.

They can accept your decisions without debating them.

Focus on getting others to join you in taking the next step.

You ratchet up huge commitment one step at a time, leaving others no way to back down.

You prove your leadership by moving people out of their comfort zone and by opening up new possibilities.

This is how teamwork creates such tremendous successes.

It is always your responsibility to guide people.

You must keep them moving forward.

You must keep them exploring new areas.

You must avoid setting limits on your goals.

The unity of the team is the source of its power.

The power of teamwork overcomes any obstacle.

If you want to be a warrior, you must be a leader.

Adjust your techniques to fit your situation.

Every situation is full of opportunities if you are open to them.

You can get people to care about what must be done.

Train yourself to inspire others.

Always use the philosophy of invasion. 6
Deep invasions concentrate your forces.
Shallow invasions scatter your forces.
When you leave your country and cross the border, you must
take control.
This is always critical ground.
You can sometimes move in any direction.
This is always intersecting ground.
You can penetrate deeply into a territory.
This is always dangerous ground.
You penetrate only a little way.
This is always easy ground.
Your retreat is closed and the path ahead tight.
This is always confined ground.
There is sometimes no place to run.
This is always deadly ground.

NATION:

The term **nation**
國 *refers to*
the productive
resources of
a country, as
distinct from
the **army** **軍** *as*
its competitive
resources.

6 Warriors train to expand their possibilities.

The bigger the challenge, the more inspiring it is.

Defending existing positions has a tendency to divide people.

When you move into new areas, you must make a serious commitment to keep going.

This initial commitment is vital.

Even when you are committed, you still have options.

Choose options that unite you with your teammates.

You can invest only so much into a specific direction.

The direction you choose must pay off.

At the beginning, progress is relatively painless.

You want to make movement as easy as possible.

You must cross certain bridges when you come to them.

Keep these critical transitions a secret.

You can run out of options.

Fight when your future depends on it.

ADAPTABILITY:

When Sun Tzu says we must know all factors to be successful, he is telling us that we have to study them, not just be exposed to them once.

[16]To use scattering terrain correctly, you must inspire your men's devotion.

On easy terrain, you must keep in close communication.

On disputed terrain, you try to hamper the enemy's progress.

On open terrain, you must carefully defend your chosen position.

On intersecting terrain, you must solidify your alliances.

On dangerous terrain, you must ensure your food supplies.

On bad terrain, you must keep advancing along the road.

On confined terrain, you must stop information leaks from your headquarters.

On deadly terrain, you must show what you can do by killing the enemy.

[25]Make your men feel like an army.

Surround them and they will defend themselves.

If they cannot avoid it, they will fight.

If they are under pressure, they will obey.

Do the right thing when you don't know your 7 different enemies' plans.

Don't attempt to meet them.

[3]You don't know the position of mountain forests, dangerous obstructions, and reservoirs?

Then you cannot march the army.

You don't have local guides?

You won't get any of the benefits of the terrain.

[7]There are many factors in war.

You may lack knowledge of any one of them.

If so, it is wrong to take a nation into war.

When you must defend your own territory, focus on shared values to maintain unity.

You must remind teammates not to take easy progress for granted.

Go after contested prizes only when you have an edge.

Know when no obstacles prevent opponents from turning on you.

Friendships are forged from shared opportunities.

The bigger the task, the more certain you must be of your resources.

When the going gets tough, look for the best way to get through it.

You must keep your vulnerabilities a secret, especially from those who can control you.

The only way to show your desperation is by making your opponents look bad.

Each member adds value to your team.

Put teammates in situations in which they must do their best.

Deny teammates the temptation of a good excuse.

Use the situation to win commitment.

7 Warriors are trained to know that they cannot advance where they cannot see.

Avoid acting out of ignorance.

You cannot let yourself be surprised by every problem, obstacle, and opponent you encounter.

You need knowledge to choose the right path.

There is no replacement for experience.

Only training teaches you how to use your position.

You need a framework for understanding your situation.

The goal of training is to make your blind spots obvious.

Only fools endanger themselves through ignorance.

[10]You must be able to control your government's war.
If you divide a big nation, it will be unable to put together a
large force.
Increase your enemy's fear of your ability.
Prevent his forces from getting together and organizing.

[14]Do the right thing and do not arrange outside alliances
before their time.
You will not have to assert your authority prematurely.
Trust only yourself and your self-interest.
This increases the enemy's fear of you.
You can make one of his allies withdraw.
His whole nation can fall.

[20]Distribute rewards without worrying about having a system.
Halt without the government's command.
Attack with the whole strength of your army.
Use your army as if it were a single man.

[24]Attack with skill.
Do not discuss it.
Attack when you have an advantage.
Do not talk about the dangers.
When you can launch your army into deadly ground, even if
it stumbles, it can still survive.
You can be weakened in a deadly battle and yet be stronger
afterward.

You must earn the trust of people in authority over you.

Divide every goal and problem into small tasks that you can complete one at a time.

You should not fear others; they should fear you.

You must undermine and divide any potential opposition.

Alliances can be extremely useful, but they can also limit many of your options.

Disagreements about direction can slow down your progress.

You must know exactly what you want out of an alliance.

Your certainty increases your rivals' uncertainty.

Your confidence can win over a rival's allies.

It can destroy a rival's credibility.

Use your own judgment about who deserves the fruits of success.

No one can force you into an opportunity.

Go forward only when you are completely committed to success.

When everyone supports a move, your success is assured.

Move forward carefully.

Bragging about future success is foolish.

Move forward when an opportunity presents itself.

Worrying about possible failure is worthless.

You will get another chance even when you take needless risks and make avoidable mistakes.

You will learn a painful but memorable lesson from picking the wrong battles.

³⁰Even a large force can fall into misfortune.
If you fall behind, however, you can still turn defeat into victory.
You must use the skills of war.
To survive, you must adapt yourself to your enemy's purpose.
You must stay with him no matter where he goes.
It may take a thousand miles to kill the general.
If you correctly understand him, you can find the skill to do it.

Manage your government correctly at the start of a war. **8**
Close your borders and tear up passports.
Block the passage of envoys.
Encourage politicians at headquarters to stay out of it.
You must use any means to put an end to politics.
Your enemy's people will leave you an opening.
You must instantly invade through it.

⁸Immediately seize a place that they love.
Do it quickly.
Trample any border to pursue the enemy.
Use your judgment about when to fight.

¹²Doing the right thing at the start of war is
like approaching a woman.
Your enemy's men must open the door.
After that, you should act like a streaking rabbit.
The enemy will be unable to catch you.

LOVE:

The concept of **love** 愛 *is consistently represented by Sun Tzu as a weakness, a dangerous excess of a necessary characteristic of a leader, caring for people.*

✦ ✦ ✦

Even when the odds are in your favor, tragedy can strike.
There are opportunities hidden in even the most painful setbacks.
You must see how your situation has changed.
After a disaster, you must learn from your opponents' philosophy.
You must measure yourself against your opponents.
You must do whatever it takes to surpass your rivals.
If you learn what they know, you can eventually succeed.

8 Warriors learn to manage those in authority over them.
You must control their access to outside information.
Control the channels of information.
Distance yourself from those concerned only with their own interests.
You must champion the shared goals of the organization.
Wait for a clear opportunity to act decisively.
Quickly take advantage of that opportunity.

You must threaten your rivals' vulnerabilities.
Speed is the key.
Don't let theoretical barriers stop you.
Your training is the key to picking the right battles.

SEDUCTION:

What situation better describes strategic competition based on positioning yourself in people's minds better than romantic seduction?

When you are in new, unfamiliar situations, you must be careful of other people's feelings.
Challenges will eventually leave you an opening.
When you see that opening, use it immediately without thinking.
Put your challenges far behind you.

Related Articles from *Sun Tzu's Playbook*

In chapter eleven, Sun Tzu explains instant situation response. To learn the step-by-step techniques involved, we recommend the Sun Tzu's Art of War Playbook *articles listed below.*

6.0 Situation Response: selecting the actions most appropriate to a situation.

6.1 Situation Recognition: situation recognition in making advances.

6.1.1 Conditioned Reflexes: how we develop automatic, instantaneous responses.

6.1.2 Prioritizing Conditions: parsing complex competitive conditions into simple responses.

6.2 Campaign Evaluation: how we justify continued investment in an ongoing campaign.

6.2.1 Campaign Flow: seeing campaigns as a series of situations that flow logically from one to another.

6.2.2 Campaign Goals: assessing the value of a campaign by a larger mission.

6.3 Campaign Patterns: how knowing campaign stages gives us insight into our situation.

6.3.1 Early-Stage Situations: the common situations that arise the earliest in campaigns.

6.3.2 Middle-Stage Situations: how progress creates transitional situations in campaigns.

6.3.3 Late-Stage Situations: understanding the final and most dangerous stages of campaigns.

6.4 Nine Situations: the nine common competitive situations.

6.4.1 Dissipating Situations: situations where defensive unity is destroyed.

6.4.2 Easy Situations: recognizing situations of easy initial progress.

6.4.3 Contentious Situations: identifying situations that invite conflict.

6.4.4 Open Situations: recognizing situations that are races without a course.

6.4.5 Intersecting Situations: recognizing situations that bring people together.

6.4.6 Serious Situations: identifying situations where resources can be cut off.

6.4.7 Difficult Situations: recognizing situations where serious barriers must be overcome.

6.4.8 Limited Situations: identifying situations defined by a bottleneck.

6.4.9 Desperate Situations: identifying situations where destruction is possible.

6.5 Nine Responses: using the best responses to the nine common competitive situations.

6.5.1 Dissipating Response: responding to dissipation by the use of offense as defense.

6.5.2 Easy Response: responding to easy situations by overcoming complacency.

6.5.3 Contentious Response: responding to contentious situations by knowing how to avoid conflict.

6.5.4 Open Response: responding to open situations by keeping up with the opposition.

6.5.5 Intersecting Response: the formation of situational alliances.

6.5.6 Serious Response: responding to serious situations by finding immediate income.

6.5.7 Difficult Response: the role of persistence in responding to difficult situations.

6.5.8 Limited Response: the need for secret speed in limited situations.

6.5.9 Desperate Response: using all our resources in responding to desperate situations.

6.6 Campaign Pause: knowing when to stop advancing a position.

Chapter 12

Attacking with Fire: The Discipline of Danger

This chapter explains the danger of fire when it is used as a weapon. A fire attack is different from attacks from regular opponents. Fire leverages the larger forces in your environment. Warriors must always be aware of their situation so that they can be on guard against becoming a target for this particular form of attack. Though the chapter deals with the danger of fire specifically, it also teaches the discipline you must maintain in the face of any type of attack.

Your vigilance against danger starts by recognizing when you might become a target. Danger can not only threaten you personally; it can threaten your resources, friends, assets, and so on. Danger from the environment doesn't arise out of thin air. You should be able to easily spot the development of threatening conditions. These dangers take time to arise, and the best method for countering them is to remove yourself from dangerous situations long before they can hurt you.

When you are threatened by danger, your safety depends upon reacting correctly. The impersonal forces of the environment and society are dangerous on their own, but the danger is magnified if you panic. Panic leaves you open to more direct attacks by other opponents. You are always threatened by changes in the environment that your opponents can use against you.

In the end, the discipline to face dangers comes from your ability to control your emotions. In this sense, fire becomes a metaphor for the fire of rage, the most dangerous element of all.

Attacking with Fire

SUN TZU SAID:

There are five targets that can be attacked with fire. 1
The first targets for fire are troops.
The second targets for fire are supplies.
The third targets for fire are supply transports.
The fourth targets for fire are storehouses.
The fifth targets for fire are camps.

FIRE:

The element of
fire 火 *is one of*
the five classi-
cal elements of
Chinese science,
but Sun Tzu
explains it using
his element of
climate.

7To make fire, people must have the resources.
To build a fire, someone must prepare the raw
materials.

9To attack with fire, it must be in the right
season.
To start a fire, someone must take the time.

11One must select the right season.
The weather must be dry.

13One must select the right time.
The season is when the grass is as high as
the side of a cart.

The Discipline of Danger

THE WARRIOR HEARS:

1 Warriors are wary of leaving targets open to attack.
People can be targets.
Resources can be targets.
Channels of support can be targets.
Long-term assets can be targets.
Communities can be targets.

People cannot create the opportunity to target you.
Rivals can only use resources found in the environment.

The climate determines when you are vulnerable.
Enemies can work to use the environment against you.

ENVIRONMENT:

The rules in this chapter apply to all weapons, but they are tailored for "environmental" weapons that leverage time.

Know when conditions are dangerous.
The fuel might exist all around you.

Know when others want to target you.
Realize that you might be sitting in a susceptible position.

¹⁵You can tell the proper days by the stars in the night sky.
You want days when the wind rises in the morning.

Everyone attacks with fire. **2**
People can create five different situations with fire and you
must be able to adjust to them.

³People can start a fire inside the enemy's camp.
Then they attack the enemy's periphery.

⁵People launch a fire attack, but the enemy remains calm.
They will then wait and not attack.

⁷The fire reaches its height.
Opponents will follow its path if they can.
If they can't follow it, they stay where they are.

¹⁰Spreading fires on the outside of camp can kill.
People can't always get fire inside the enemy's camp.
They take their time in spreading it.

TRANSFORM:

The character **transform** 變 *also means* **change**, *and it is the key aspect of climate, just as* **form** 形f *is the key aspect of ground.*

¹³People set fire when the wind is at their
back.
They won't attack into the wind.
Daytime winds last a long time.
Night winds fade quickly.

Warriors know when climate changes are going against them.
They can feel the danger in the shifts in the wind.

2 Warriors know that a threat can come from any direction.
You must recognize the five different forms that environmental
threats take and know how to counter them.

The leader of a group can have a problem.
Then enemies will attempt to pick off his supporters.

If you remain calm during crises, you are safe.
The real danger is when you panic.

Every crisis will reach a peak.
During these moments, avoid leaving your opponents an opening.
Without an opening, they cannot bring you down.

People can trigger little irritations all around you.
This is common when rivals cannot hurt you directly.
You must defend yourself for a long time.

WEAPONS:

You are in danger when the climate goes against
you.
When your luck changes, you are safe.
A well-known reputation can last a long time.
A little-known reputation can be changed easily.

*Sun Tzu does
not teach about
using specific
weapons be-
cause he knew
that all physical
weapons would
become out-
dated.*

17Every army must know how to adjust to the five possible
attacks by fire.
Use many men to guard against them.

People who use fire to assist their attacks are clever. 3
Water can add force to an attack.
People can also use water to disrupt an enemy.
It does not, however, take his resources.

You win in battle by getting the opportunity to attack. 4
It is dangerous if you fail to study how to accomplish this
achievement.
As commander, you cannot waste your opportunities.

4We say:
A wise leader plans success.
A good general studies it.
If there is little to be gained, don't act.
If there is little to win, do not use your men.
If there is no danger, don't fight.

EMOTION:

*The personal
characteristic
associated with
climate is emo-
tion, and fire
is specifically
associated with*
anger 愠 *and*
fury 怒.

10As leader, you cannot let your anger inter-
fere with the success of your forces.
As commander, you cannot let yourself
become enraged before you go to battle.
Join the battle only when it is in your advantage to act.
If there is no advantage in joining a battle,
stay put.

You can defend against any form of attack if you know what to expect.
All you need is vigilance.

3 Warriors are wary of opponents who use the environment.
Changes in the environment can add ferocity to any attack.
Your progress is easy to stop if the climate is against you.
Forces in the environment can seriously damage you.

4 Warriors are always looking for paths to move forward.
You leave yourself open to attack when you fail to maintain the initiative.
You must grab opportunities when you see them.

Open your eyes.
You lead by virtue of your good judgment.
Others listen to you because they respect your knowledge.
The benefit of your actions must outweigh their cost.
Useless battles undermine everyone's support.
Avoid conflict unless it is more dangerous not to fight.

Warriors know how to control their emotions so that they can make good decisions.
Your decision to meet a challenge must be made with a clear head and a quiet heart.
You gain nothing by lashing out in anger.
If you have nothing to gain, you must hold your peace.

RESPONSE:

If people are not taught how to respond to situations, they respond emotionally. The goal of strategy is to respond appropriately.

[14]Anger can change back into happiness.

Rage can change back into joy.

A nation once destroyed cannot be brought back to life.

Dead men do not return to the living.

[18]This fact must make a wise leader cautious.

A good general is on guard.

[20]Your philosophy must be to keep the nation peaceful and the army intact.

♦ ♦ ♦

RECOVER:

The character **recover 復** *indicates the ability to return to a previous state, which is easy with emotional (climate) states, but impossible in matters of life and death.*

Emotions change like the weather.

Today's enemy can become tomorrow's friend.

When actions are destructive, you cannot take them back.

What you lose, you can lose forever.

You must be sensitive about every action you choose.

You must also be sensitive to threats.

Your path to success depends on avoiding unnecessary conflict while you protect yourself.

Decisions:

Mastering the science of strategy leads to better decisions because you will know a whole range of responses and will have to rely less on your emotions.

Related Articles from *Sun Tzu's Playbook*

In chapter twelve, Sun Tzu discusses the use of environmental weapons. To learn the step-by-step techniques involved, we recommend the Sun Tzu's Art of War Playbook *articles listed below.*

9.0 Understanding Vulnerability: the use of common environmental attacks.

9.1 Climate Vulnerability: our vulnerability to environmental crises arising from change.

9.1.1 Climate Rivals: how changing conditions create opponents.

9.1.2 Threat Development: how changing conditions create environmental threats.

9.2 Points of Vulnerability: our points of vulnerability during an environmental crisis.

9.2.1 Personnel Risk: the vulnerability of key individuals.

9.2.2 Immediate Resource Risk: the vulnerability of the resources required for immediate use.

9.2.3 Transportation/Communication Risk: how firestorms choke normal channels of movement and communication.

9.2.4 Asset Risk: the threats to our fixed assets.

9.2.5 Organizational Risk: targeting the roles and responsibilities within an organization.

9.3 Crisis Leadership: maintaining the support of our supporters during attacks.

9.3.1 Mutual Danger: how we use mutual danger to create mutual strength.

9.3.2 Message Control: communication methods to use during a crisis.

9.4 Crisis Defense: how vulnerabilities are exploited and defended during a crisis.

9.4.1 Division Defense: preventing organizational division during a crisis.

9.4.2 Panic Defense: preventing the mistakes arising from panic during a crisis.

9.4.3 Defending Openings: how to defend openings created by a crisis.

9.4.4 Defending Alliances: dealing with guilt by association.

9.4.5 Defensive Balance: using short-term conditions to tip the balance in a crisis.

9.5 Crisis Exploitation: how to successfully use an opponent's crisis.

9.5.1 Adversarial Opportunities: how our opponents' crises can create opportunities.

9.5.2 Avoiding Emotion: the danger of exploiting environmental vulnerabilities for purely emotion reasons.

9.6 Constant Vigilance: where to focus our attention to preserve our positions.

Chapter 13

用 間

Using Spies: A Network of Sources

You have probably heard that success depends less on what you know than on who you know. In classical strategy, this idea is a little more sophisticated. Sun Tzu teaches that what you know depends on who you know. Information is the source of all strategy, but you can only get the most valuable information from having the right contacts. Strategy replaces force and effort with good information—which you obtain through cultivating the right sources.

The world is a dangerous place. Without the right information, you cannot properly prepare for its dangers. Most people spend too little time, effort, and money on getting good information. Warriors are different from ordinary people because they place a premium on staying informed. You must build and maintain a network of personal contacts if you want to be successful.

Information can be misleading, especially when it comes from only one type of source. Good strategy requires that warriors build a wide variety of contacts to provide a well-rounded view of every situation. Sun Tzu teaches specifically that five different types of sources are needed to create a complete view.

Developing and maintaining a good network of sources requires a special set of skills. Without the right social skills, you will never get the information you need. Without the information you need, you cannot develop a successful strategy. In many ways, Sun Tzu saves his most important lessons for the end of his book.

Using Spies

All successful armies require thousands of men. 1
They invade and march thousands of miles.
Whole families are destroyed.
Other families must be heavily taxed.
Every day, a large amount of money must be spent.

⁶Internal and external events force people to
move.
They are unable to work while on the road.
They are unable to find and hold a useful job.
This affects 70 percent of thousands of families.

¹⁰You can watch and guard for years.
Then a single battle can determine victory in
a day.
Despite this, bureaucrats worship the value
of their salary money too dearly.
They remain ignorant of the enemy's condi-
tion.
The result is cruel.

WASTE:

The concept of
waste 費 *is the*
economic result
of substitut-
ing material
resources for
knowledge or
information
resources.

208 *The Art of War 13: Using Spies*

A Network of Sources

THE WARRIOR HEARS:

1 Warriors know their success depends upon many people.
Meeting challenges and going the distance don't assure success.
The risks are real.
Everyone makes sacrifices.
No matter how much you spend, you cannot buy your victories.

All people get pushed around by events beyond their control.
At some point, you will be forced to go job hunting.
You will have periods when you cannot find work.
The competitive job market makes nothing certain.

It can take years for an opportunity to appear.
You must prepare for a decisive event that changes your life.
True success will never come from being a cog in the system and saving your money.
Money is worthless if you remain ignorant of your opportunities.
You will miss out.

CIRCLE:

This chapter completes a circle. The book begins with analysis, but analysis begins with your information sources.

[15]They are not leaders of men.
They are not servants of the state.
They are not masters of victory.

[18]People need an intelligent leader and a worthy commander.
You must move your troops to the right places to beat others.
You must accomplish your attack and escape unharmed.
This requires foreknowledge.
You can obtain foreknowledge.
You can't get it from demons or spirits.
You can't see it from professional experience.
You can't check it with analysis.
You can only get it from other people.
You must always know the enemy's situation.

You must use five types of spies. 2
You need local spies.
You need inside spies.
You need double agents.
You need doomed spies.
You need surviving spies.

[7]You need all five types of spies.
No one must discover your methods.
You will then be able to put together a true picture.
This is the commander's most valuable resource.

[11]You need local spies.
Get them by hiring people from the countryside.

SPIES:

Though translated here as **spies**, *the character* 間 *specifically means a* **between space**, *as we might say* a **go-between** *or a* **channel of information.**

Without the right knowledge, you will always be a follower.
Without the right knowledge, you will never take the lead.
Without knowledge, you will never succeed.

Others must see you as wise and skilled.
You must know enough to do the right thing at the right time.
You must know how to make progress in the face of danger.
You must know what others are thinking.
That information is available to you.
There is no magic in foreseeing the future.
You cannot trust in just your past experience.
Knowledge never comes from facts alone.
Only people can tell you what they are planning.
You must understand the positions others are in.

2 Warriors develop a five information channels.
You need information on your environment.
You need information on leaders.
You need information on your rivals.
You need to transmit misleading information.
You need timely information.

POWER:

*Knowledge is power. Strategy depends on secret knowledge. For example, the code **WEL96543** discounts your first order at our Strategy Store.*

A single viewpoint is misleading.
People will tell you just what you want to hear.
You must overcome your preconceptions to see the truth.
You must protect your information sources and methods.

Some people know your battleground better than you do.
You must make contact with people with experience.

¹³You need inside spies.
Win them by subverting government officials.

¹⁵You need double agents.
Discover enemy agents and convert them.

¹⁷You need doomed spies.
Deceive professionals into being captured.
Let them know your orders.
They will then take those orders to your enemy.

²¹You need surviving spies.
Someone must return with a report.

Your job is to build a complete army. 3
No relations are as intimate as the ones with spies.
No rewards are too generous for spies.
No work is as secret as that of spies.

⁵If you aren't clever and wise, you can't use spies.
If you aren't fair and just, you can't use spies.
If you can't see the small subtleties, you won't get the truth
from spies.

⁸Pay attention to small, trifling details!
Spies are helpful in every area.

Insiders are close to decision-makers.
Only insiders know how those in authority think.

Identify your rivals' information sources.
These people will allow you to understand your rivals' methods.

You must sacrifice some information channels.
The goal is to mislead others about your intentions.
You need to control people's perceptions.
Once you have misled a source, you cannot use him or her again.

Finally, there are sources you must protect.
You need critical news immediately.

3 Warriors seek out the whole story.
You must make your information sources into your best friends.
You must be willing to pay for good information.
You need to know what no one else knows.

You must learn what makes sense and what doesn't.
You must weigh each fact without prejudice.
You must especially pay attention to small details because details
are difficult to fake.

The smallest minutiae give the truest picture.
Every scrap of information is important.

¹⁰Spies are the first to hear information, so they must not spread information.
Spies who give your location or talk to others must be terminated along with those to whom they have talked.

You may want to attack an army's position. 4
You may want to attack a certain fortification.
You may want to eliminate people in a certain place.
You must first know the guarding general.
You must know his left and right flanks.
You must know his hierarchy.
You must know the way in.
You must know where different people are stationed.
You must demand this information from your spies.

¹⁰You want to know the enemy spies in order to convert them into your men.
You find sources of information and bribe them.
You must bring them in with you.
You must obtain them as double agents and use them as your emissaries.

¹⁴Do this correctly and carefully.
You can contact both local and inside spies and obtain their support.
Do this correctly and carefully.
You create doomed spies by deceiving professionals.
You can use them to give false information.
Do this correctly and carefully.
You must have surviving spies capable of bringing you information at the right time.

You must trust your sources to get you information quickly before its value disappears.

If your contacts give out confidential information about you, they do you more harm than good.

4 Warriors need specific information to take specific actions.

Your ability to move forward always depends upon information.

Windows of opportunity open only at specific places and times.

When you know about powerful people, you know how to behave.

When you know about specific barriers, you can overcome them.

When you tackle a specific organization, you can outmaneuver it.

Your knowledge is the key that opens the door.

Your knowledge is the secret to avoiding conflict.

You must develop contacts to get this information.

The best place to start developing contacts is with people who are in contact with your rivals.

They must find dealing with you rewarding.

You must befriend these people.

You can use these sources to get information from your opponents and to misinform them.

Do not take chances with valuable sources.

You need to know people with special expertise and people who know people with special expertise.

It takes work to build an information network.

You sometimes need to sacrifice an information source.

Providing misinformation can be extremely valuable.

You must pick the right situations.

You must protect key information sources because only they can get you the most valuable news.

²¹These are the five different types of intelligence work.
You must be certain to master them all.
You must be certain to create double agents.
You cannot afford to be too cost conscious in creating these
double agents.

This technique created the success of ancient Shang. 5
This is how the Shang held their dynasty.

³You must always be careful of your success.
Learn from Lu Ya of Shang.

⁵Be a smart commander and a good general.
You do this by using your best and brightest
people for spying.
This is how you achieve the greatest success.
This is how you meet the necessities of war.
The whole army's position and ability to
move depends on these spies.

REVERSE:

*The concept of
reversal 反 is
central to Sun
Tzu's strategy
since every situ-
ation depends
on generating its
opposite, in this
case, undermin-
ing an enemy's
knowledge.*

You must suspect information that comes from only one source.
Act only on information that you can verify.
You must especially know your rivals' points of view.
Most people spend too little time and effort learning what their rivals know.

5 Warriors throughout history have depended on information. History's conquerors have been information magicians.

You can be as successful as any person in history.
All successful people use the same basic strategy.

Make good choices and provide dependable leadership.
Winning is much more a matter of information than of strength.
Information helps you achieve any goal.
You can consistently choosing the right challenges.
Your position in the world and your progress through life depend on your network of sources.

EXCESS:

Lu Ya was an officer under a Shang-dynasty tyrant who got inside a tyrant's information network to overthrow him. See our **Amazing Secrets** *book for more.*

♦ ♦ ♦

♦ ♦ ♦

Related Articles from *Sun Tzu's Playbook*

In his final chapter, Sun Tzu explains how to use information channels. To learn the step-by-step techniques involved, we recommend the Sun Tzu's Art of War Playbook *articles listed below.*

2.0.0 Developing Perspective: adding depth to competitive analysis.

2.1 Information Value: knowledge and communication as the basis of strategy.

2.1.1 Information Limits: making good decisions with limited information.

2.1.3 Strategic Deception: misinformation and disinformation in competition.

2.1.4 Surprise: how the creation of surprise depends on the nature of information.

2.2 Information Gathering: gathering competitive information.

2.2.1 Personal Relationships: why information depends on personal relationships.

2.2.3 Standard Terminology: how mental models must be shared to enable communication.

2.3 Personal Interactions: making progress through personal interactions.

2.3.4 Using Questions: using questions in gathering information and predicting reactions.

2.3.5 Infinite Loops: predicting reactions on the basis of the "you-know-that-I-know-that-you-know" problem.

2.3.6 Promises and Threats: the use of promises and threats as strategic moves.

2.4 Contact Networks: the range of contacts needed to create perspective.

2.4.1 Ground Perspective: getting information on a new competitive arena.

2.4.2 Climate Perspective: getting perspective on temporary external conditions.

2.4.3 Command Perspective: developing sources for understanding decision-makers.

2.4.4 Methods Perspective: developing contacts who understand best practices.

2.4.5 Mission Perspective: how we develop and use a perspective on motivation.

2.5 The Big Picture: building big-picture strategic awareness.

2.6 Knowledge Leverage: getting competitive value out of knowledge.

2.7 Information Secrecy: defining the role of secrecy in relationships.

Glossary of Key Strategic Concepts

This glossary is keyed to the most common English words used in the translation of *The Art of War*. Those terms only capture the strategic concepts generally. Though translated as English nouns, verbs, adverbs, or adjectives, the Chinese characters on which they are based are totally conceptual, not parts of speech. For example, the character for CONFLICT is translated as the noun "conflict," as the verb "fight," and as the adjective "disputed." Ancient written Chinese was a conceptual language, not a spoken one. More like mathematical terms, these concepts are primarily defined by the strict structure of their relationships with other concepts. The Chinese names shown in parentheses with the characters are primarily based on Pinyin, but we occasionally use Cantonese terms to make each term unique.

ADVANCE (JEUN 進): to move into new GROUND; to expand your POSITION; to move forward in a campaign; the opposite of FLEE.

ADVANTAGE, *benefit* (LI 利): an opportunity arising from having a better POSITION relative to an ENEMY; an opening left by an ENEMY; a STRENGTH that matches against an ENEMY'S WEAKNESS; where fullness meets emptiness; a desirable characteristic of a strategic POSITION.

AIM, *vision*, *foresee* (JIAN 見): FOCUS on a specific ADVANTAGE, opening, or opportunity; predicting movements of an ENEMY; a skill of a LEADER in observing CLIMATE.

ANALYSIS, *plan* (GAI 計): a comparison of relative POSITION; the examination of the five factors that define a strategic POSITION; a combination of KNOWLEDGE and VISION; the ability to see through DECEPTION.

ARMY: see WAR.

ATTACK, *invade* (GONG 攻): a movement to new GROUND; advancing a strategic POSITION; action against an ENEMY in the sense of moving into his GROUND; opposite of DEFEND; does not necessarily mean CONFLICT.

BAD, *ruined* (PI 坏): a condition of the GROUND that makes ADVANCE difficult; destroyed; terrain that is broken and difficult to traverse; one of the nine situations or types of terrain.

BARRICADED: see OBSTACLES.

BATTLE (ZHAN 戰): to challenge; to engage an ENEMY; generically, to meet a challenge; to choose a confrontation with an ENEMY at a specific time and place; to focus all your resources on a task; to establish superiority in a POSITION; to challenge an ENEMY to increase CHAOS; that which is CONTROLLED by SURPRISE; one of the four forms of ATTACK; the response to a DESPERATE SITUATION; character meaning was originally "big meeting," though later took on the meaning "big weapon"; not necessarily CONFLICT.

BRAVERY, *courage* (YONG 勇): the ability to face difficult choices; the character quality that deals with the changes of CLIMATE; courage of conviction; willingness to act on vision; one of the six characteristics of a leader.

BREAK, *broken*, *divided* (PO 破): to DIVIDE what is COMPLETE; the absence of a UNITING PHILOSOPHY; the opposite of UNITY.

CALCULATE, *count* (SHU 數): mathematical comparison of quantities and qualities; a measurement of DISTANCE or troop size.

CHANGE, *transform* (BIAN 變): transition from one CONDITION to another; the ability to adapt to different situations; a natural characteristic of CLIMATE.

CHAOS, *disorder* (JUAN 亂): CONDITIONS that cannot be FORESEEN; the natural state of confusion arising from BATTLE; one of six weaknesses of an organization; the opposite of CONTROL.

CLAIM, *position*, *form* (XING 形): to use the GROUND; a shape or specific condition of GROUND; the GROUND that you CONTROL; to use the benefits of the GROUND; the formations of troops; one of the four key skills in making progress.

CLIMATE, *heaven* (TIAN 天): the passage of time; the realm of uncontrollable CHANGE; divine providence; the weather; trends that CHANGE over time; generally, the future; what one must AIM at in the future; one of five key factors in ANALYSIS; the opposite of GROUND.

COMMAND (LING 令): to order or the act of ordering subordinates; the decisions of a LEADER; the creation of METHODS.

COMPETITION: see WAR.

COMPLETE: see UNITY.

CONDITION: see GROUND.

CONFINED, *surround* (WEI 圍): to encircle; a SITUATION or STAGE in which your options are limited; the proper tactic for dealing with an ENEMY that is ten times smaller; to seal off a smaller ENEMY; the characteristic of a STAGE in which a larger FORCE can be attacked by a smaller one; one of nine SITUATIONS or STAGES.

CONFLICT, *fight* (ZHENG 爭): to contend; to dispute; direct confrontation of arms with an ENEMY; highly desirable GROUND that creates disputes; one of nine types of GROUND, terrain, or stages.

CONSTRICTED, *narrow* (AI 狹): a confined space or niche; one of six field positions; the limited extreme of the dimension distance; the opposite of SPREAD-OUT.

CONTROL, *govern* (CHI 治): to manage situations; to overcome disorder; the opposite of CHAOS.

DANGEROUS: see SERIOUS.

DANGERS, *adverse* (AK 阨): a condition that makes it difficult to ADVANCE; one of three dimensions used to evaluate advantages; the dimension with the extreme field POSITIONS of ENTANGLING and SUPPORTING.

DEATH, *desperate* (SI 死): to end or the end of life or efforts; an extreme situation in which the only option is BATTLE; one of nine STAGES or types of TERRAIN; one of five types of SPIES; opposite of SURVIVE.

DECEPTION, *bluffing, illusion* (GUI 詭): to control perceptions; to control information; to mislead an ENEMY; an attack on an opponent's AIM; the characteristic of war that confuses perceptions.

DEFEND (SHOU 守): to guard or to hold a GROUND; to remain in a POSITION; the opposite of **ATTACK.**

DETOUR (YU 迂): the indirect or unsuspected path to a POSITION; the more difficult path to ADVANTAGE; the route that is not DIRECT.

DIRECT, *straight* (JIK 直): a straight or obvious path to a goal; opposite of DETOUR.

DISTANCE, *distant* (YUAN 遠): the space separating GROUND; to be remote from the current location; to occupy POSITIONS that are not close to one another; one of six field positions; one of the three dimensions for evaluating opportunities; the emptiness of space.

DIVIDE, *separate* (FEN 分): to break apart a larger force; to separate from a larger group; the opposite of JOIN and FOCUS.

DOUBLE AGENT, *reverse* (FAN 反): to turn around in direction; to change a situation; to switch a person's allegiance; one of five types of spies.

EASY, *light* (QING 輕): to require little effort; a SITUATION that requires little effort; one of nine STAGES or types of terrain; opposite of SERIOUS.

EMOTION, *feeling* (XIN 心): an unthinking reaction to AIM, a necessary element to inspire MOVES; a component of esprit de corps; never a sufficient cause for ATTACK.

ENEMY, *competitor* (DIK 敵): one who makes the same CLAIM; one with a similar GOAL; one with whom comparisons of capabilities are made.

ENTANGLING, *hanging* (GUA 懸): a POSITION that cannot be returned to; any CONDITION that leaves no easy place to go; one of six field positions.

EVADE, *avoid* (BI 避): the tactic used by small competitors when facing large opponents.

FALL APART, *collapse* (BENG 崩): to fail to execute good decisions; to fail to use a CONSTRICTED POSITION; one of six weaknesses of an organization.

FALL DOWN, *sink* (HAAM 陷): to fail to make good decisions; to MOVE from a SUPPORTING POSITION; one of six weaknesses of organizations.

FEELINGS, *affection, love* (CHING 情): the bonds of relationship; the result of a shared PHILOSOPHY; requires management.

FIGHT, *struggle* (DOU 鬥): to engage in CONFLICT; to face difficulties.

FIRE (HUO 火): an environmental weapon; a universal analogy for all weapons.

FLEE, *retreat, northward* (BEI 北): to abandon a POSITION; to surrender GROUND; one of six weaknesses of an ARMY; opposite of ADVANCE.

FOCUS, *concentrate* (ZHUAN 專): to bring resources together at a given time; to UNITE forces for a purpose; an attribute of having a shared PHILOSOPHY; the opposite of *divide*.

FORCE (LEI 力): power in the simplest sense; a GROUP of people bound by UNITY and FOCUS; the relative balance of STRENGTH in opposition to WEAKNESS.

FORESEE: see AIM.

FULLNESS: see STRENGTH.

GENERAL: see LEADER.

GOAL: see PHILOSOPHY.

GROUND, *situation, stage* (DI 地): the earth; a specific place; a specific condition; the place one competes; the prize of competition; one of five key factors in competitive analysis; the opposite of CLIMATE.

GROUPS, *troops* (DUI 隊): a number of people united under a shared PHILOSOPHY; human resources of an organization; one of the five targets of fire attacks.

INSIDE, *internal* (NEI 内): within a TERRITORY or organization; an insider; one of five types of spies; opposite of OUTSIDE.

INTERSECTING, *highway* (QU 衢): a SITUATION or GROUND that allows you to JOIN; one of nine types of terrain.

JOIN (HAP 合): to unite; to make allies; to create a larger FORCE; opposite of DIVIDE.

KNOWLEDGE, *listening* (ZHI 知): to have information; the result of listening; the first step in advancing a POSITION; the basis of strategy.

LAX, *loosen* (SHII 弛): too easygoing; lacking discipline; one of six weaknesses of an army.

LEADER, *general, commander* (JIANG 將): the decision-maker in a competitive unit; one who LISTENS and AIMS; one who manages TROOPS; superior of officers and men; one of the five key factors in analysis; the conceptual opposite of SYSTEM, the established methods, which do not require decisions.

LEARN, *compare* (XIAO 效): to evaluate the relative qualities of ENEMIES.

LISTEN, *obey* (TING 聽): to gather KNOWLEDGE; part of ANALYSIS.

LISTENING: see KNOWLEDGE.

LOCAL, *countryside* (XIANG 鄉): the nearby GROUND; to have KNOWLEDGE of a specific GROUND; one of five types of SPIES.

MARSH (ZE 澤): GROUND where foot-ing is unstable; one of the four types of GROUND; analogy for uncertain situations.

METHOD: see SYSTEM.

MISSION: see PHILOSOPHY.

MOMENTUM, *influence* (SHI 勢): the FORCE created by SURPRISE set up by STANDARDS; used with TIMING.

MOUNTAINS, *hill, peak* (SHAN 山): uneven GROUND; one of four types of GROUND; an analogy for all unequal SITUATIONS.

MOVE, *march, act* (HANG 行): action toward a position or goal.

NATION (GUO 國): the state; the productive part of an organization; the seat of political power; the entity that controls an ARMY or competitive part of the organization.

OBSTACLES, *barricaded* (XIAN 險): to have barriers; one of the three characteristics of the GROUND; one of six field positions; as a field position, opposite of UNOBSTRUCTED.

OPEN, *meeting, crossing* (JIAO 來): to share the same GROUND without conflict; to come together; a SITUATION that encourages a race; one of nine TERRAINS or STAGES.

OPPORTUNITY: see ADVANTAGE.

OUTMANEUVER (SOU 走): to go astray; to be FORCED into a WEAK POSITION; one of six weaknesses of an army.

OUTSIDE, *external* (WAI 外): not within a TERRITORY or ARMY; one who has a different perspective; one who offers an objective view; opposite of INTERNAL.

PHILOSOPHY, *mission, goals* (TAO 道): the shared GOALS that UNITE an ARMY; a system of thought; a shared viewpoint; literally "the way"; a way to work together; one of the five factors in ANALYSIS.

PLATEAU (LIU 陸): a type of GROUND without defects; an analogy for any equal, solid, and certain SITUATION; the best place for competition; one of the four types of GROUND.

RESOURCES, *provisions* (LIANG 糧): necessary supplies, most commonly food; one of the five targets of fire attacks.

RESTRAINT: see TIMING.

REWARD, *treasure, money* (BAO 賞): profit; wealth; the necessary compensation for competition; a necessary ingredient for

VICTORY; VICTORY must pay.

SCATTER, *dissipating* (SAN 散): to disperse; to lose UNITY; the pursuit of separate GOALS as opposed to a central MISSION; a situation that causes a FORCE to scatter; one of nine conditions or types of terrain.

SERIOUS, *heavy* (CHONG 重): any task requiring effort and skill; a SITUATION where resources are running low when you are deeply committed to a campaign or heavily invested in a project; a situation where opposition within an organization mounts; one of nine STAGES or types of TERRAIN.

SIEGE (GONG CHENG 攻城): to move against entrenched positions; any movement against an ENEMY'S STRENGTH; literally "strike city"; one of the four forms of attack; the least desirable form of attack.

SITUATION: see GROUND.

SPEED, *hurry* (SAI 馳): to MOVE over GROUND quickly; the ability to ADVANCE POSITIONS in a minimum of time; needed to take advantage of a window of opportunity.

SPREAD-OUT, *wide* (GUANG 廣): a surplus of DISTANCE; one of the six GROUND POSITIONS; opposite of CONSTRICTED.

SPY, *conduit, go-between* (GAAN 間): a source of information; a channel of communication; literally, an "opening between."

STAGE: see GROUND.

STANDARD, *proper, correct* (JANG 正): the expected behavior; the standard approach; proven methods; the opposite of SURPRISE; together with SURPRISE creates MOMENTUM.

STOREHOUSE, *house* (KU 庫): a place where resources are stockpiled; one of the five targets for fire attacks.

STORES, *accumulate, savings* (JI 糧): resources that have been stored; any type of inventory; one of the five targets of fire attacks.

STRENGTH, *fullness, satisfaction* (SAT 壹): wealth or abundance or resources; the state of being crowded; the opposite of XU, empty.

SUPPLY WAGONS, *transport* (ZI 輜): the movement of RESOURCES through DISTANCE; one of the five targets of fire attacks.

SUPPORT, *supporting* (ZHII 支): to prop up; to enhance; a GROUND POSITION that you cannot leave without losing STRENGTH; one of six field positions; the opposite extreme of ENTANGLING.

SURPRISE, *unusual, strange* (QI 奇): the unexpected; the innovative; the opposite of STANDARD; together with STANDARDS creates MOMENTUM.

SURROUND: see CONFINED.

SURVIVE, *live, birth* (SHAANG 生): the state of being created, started, or beginning; the state of living or surviving; a temporary condition of fullness; one of five types of spies; the opposite of DEATH.

SYSTEM, *method* (FA 法): a set of procedures; a group of techniques; steps to accomplish a GOAL; one of the five key factors in analysis; the realm of groups who must follow procedures; the opposite of the LEADER.

TERRITORY, *terrain*: see GROUND.

TIMING, *restraint* (JIE 節): to withhold action until the proper time; to release tension; a companion concept to MOMENTUM.

TROOPS: see GROUPS.

UNITY, *whole, oneness* (YI 一): the characteristic of a GROUP that shares a PHILOSOPHY; the lowest number; a GROUP that acts as a unit; the opposite of DIVIDED.

UNOBSTRUCTED, *expert* (TONG 通): without obstacles or barriers; GROUND that allows easy movement; open to new ideas; one of six field positions; opposite of OBSTRUCTED.

VICTORY, *win, winning* (SING 勝): success in an endeavor; getting a reward; serving your mission; an event that produces more than it consumes; to make a profit.

WAR, *competition, army* (BING 兵): a dynamic situation in which POSITIONS can be won or lost; a contest in which a REWARD can be won; the conditions under which the rules of strategy work.

WATER, *river* (SHUI 水): a fast-changing GROUND; fluid CONDITIONS; one of four types of GROUND; an analogy for change.

WEAKNESS, *emptiness, need* (XU 處): the absence of people or resources; devoid of FORCE; the point of ATTACK for an ADVANTAGE; a characteristic of GROUND that enables SPEED; poor; the opposite of STRENGTH.

WIN, *winning*: see VICTORY.

WIND, *fashion, custom* (FENG 風): the pressure of environmental forces.

Index of Topics in *The Art of War*

This index identifies significant topics, keyed to the chapters, block numbers (big numbers in text), and line numbers (tiny numbers). The format is chapter:block.lines.

About the Author

Gary Gagliardi

This book's award-winning translator and primary author, Gary Gagliardi, is America's leading authority on Sun Tzu's *The Art of War*. A frequent guest on radio and television talk shows, Gary has written over wenty books on strategy. Ten of his books on Sun Tzu's methods have won award recognition in business, self-help, career, sports, philosophy, multicultural, and youth nonfiction categories.

Gary began studying Sun Tzu's philosophy over thirty years ago. His understanding of strategy was proven in the business world, where his software company became one of the Inc. 500 fastest-growing companies in America and won numerous business awards. After selling his software company, Gary began writing about and teaching Sun Tzu's strategic philosophy full time.

He has spoken all over the world on a variety of topics concerning competition, from modern technology to ancient history. His books have been translated into many languages, including Japanese, Thai, Korean, Russian, Indonesian, and Spanish.

Today he splits his time between Seattle and Las Vegas, living with his wife, Rebecca, and travels extensively for speaking engagements all over the world.

garyg@suntzus.com

@strategygary

Want to learn more about Sun Tzu's strategy?

SUNTZUS.COM

SCIENCE OF STRATEGY INSTITUTE

eBooks

Audio books

Audio seminars

Online training

Art of War and Strategy Books By Gary Gagliardi

Sun Tzu's Art of War Rule Book in Nine Volumes

Sun Tzu's The Art of War Plus The Art of Sales: Strategy for the Sales Warrior

9 Formulas for Business Success: the Science of Strategy

The Golden Key to Strategy: Everyday Strategy for Everyone

The Art of War Plus The Chinese Revealed

The Art of War Plus The Art of Management: Straegy for Management Warriors

Art of War for Warrior Marketing: Strategy for Conquering Markets

The Art of War Plus The Art of Politics: Strategy for Campaigns (with Shawn
Frost)

Making Money By Speaking: The Spokesperson Strategy

The Warrior Class: 306 Lessons in Strategy

The Art of War for the Business Warrior: Strategy for Entrepreneurs

The Art of War Plus The Warrior's Apprentice: Strategy for Teens

The Art of War Plus Strategy for Sales Managers: Strategy for Sales Groups

The Ancient Bing-fa: Martial Arts Strategy

Strategy Against Terror: Ancient Wisdom for Today's War

The Art of War Plus The Art of Career Building: Strategy for Promotion

Sun Tzu's Art of War Plus Parenting Teens

The Art of War Plus Its Amazing Secrets: The Keys to Ancient Chinese Science

Art of War Plus Art of Love: Strategy for Romance

72011505R00126

Made in the USA
Columbia, SC
13 June 2017